ETs and UFOs

ETs
AND
UFOs

ARE THEY REAL?

BY LARRY KETTELKAMP

MORROW JUNIOR BOOKS

New York

Text copyright © 1996 by Larry Kettelkamp

Library of Congress Cataloging-in-Publication Data
Kettelkamp, Larry.
ETs and UFOs: are they real?/by Larry Kettelkamp.
p. cm.
Summary: An overview of reported sightings of UFOs and reports of encounters with aliens as well as the agencies whose work is to monitor and investigate such claims.
Includes bibliographical references and index.
ISBN 0-688-12868-8
1. Unidentified flying objects—Juvenile literature.
2. Human-alien encounters—Juvenile literature.
[1. Unidentified flying objects. 2. Human-alien encounters. 3. Extraterrestrial beings.] I. Title.
TL789.2.K48 1996 001.9'42—dc20 96-6825 CIP AC

The author wishes to thank the following persons for contributing materials and offering helpful suggestions: Pat Marcattilio, Thomas Benson, Robert Durant, Joe Stefula, George Hansen, Mindy Gerber, Arthur Wagner, Tom Carey, Glenn Dennis, Jenny Randles, John Schuessler, Kathy Schuessler, Don Ecker, Jack Kasher, Mark Carlotto, Walter Webb, Timothy Goode, Betty Hill, Debbie Jordan, Kathy Mitchell, Raymond Fowler, Jack Weiner, Jim Weiner, Charlie Foltz, Jesse Marcel, Jr.

Special gratitude is extended to those listed above who are members of the New Jersey and Pennsylvania UFO Study Group of MUFON, and to the UFO Enigma Museum, Roswell, New Mexico.

Picture Credits

Mark Carlotto, p. 13; Glenn Dennis, p. 43; Robert Durant, p. 28; Don Ecker/*UFO Magazine*, p. 9; Charlie Foltz, p. 64; Timothy Goode, p. 27; Harvard University Observatory, p. 80; Betty Hill, pp. 51, 52 (both), 53; Debbie Jordan, pp. 67, 69 (left); Larry Kettelkamp, pp. 7, 29, 46, 47, 73 (both); Jesse Marcel, Jr., p. 36 (bottom); Kathy Mitchell, p. 69 (right); NASA, pp. 4, 6 (both), 10; Jenny Randles, pp. 19, 20, 23 (both), 24, 25; *Roswell Daily Record*, pp. 32, 34; Kathy Schuessler, p. 15; UFO Enigma Museum, pp. 39, 41 (both); UTA Libraries, p. 36 (top); Walter Webb, pp. 55, 56, 58, 59; Jack Weiner, jacket (both), pp. 61, 63 (both); Jim Weiner, p. 62 (both) *to Pat Marcattilio, who generously lent unlimited time, encouragement, and resource materials to help make this project possible*

CONTENTS

ETs and UFOs

INTRODUCTION

SINCE ANCIENT DAYS THERE have been stories of unearthly objects in the sky. Some two thousand years ago the author of an epic Indian poem called *Mahabharata* wrote: "A blazing missile...of the radiance of smokeless fire was discharged.... This missile spins, radiates light, is operated by a circular reflecting device, and leaves a wake of great, scorching heat." In the Bible the prophet Ezekiel spoke of creatures appearing from a whirlwind and a cloud of fire: "They four had one likeness: and their appearance and their work was as it were a wheel in the middle of a wheel.... As for their rings, they were so high that they were dreadful.... And when the living creatures went, the wheels went with them: and when the living creatures were lifted up from the earth, the wheels were lifted up."

An English manuscript from the year 1290 tells of

two monks who rushed into a monastery, crying that there was "a great portent outside...a large, round silver thing like a disc [that] flew slowly over them and excited the greatest terror." In 1882, observers at England's Greenwich Observatory watched a huge "torpedo" ascending to about two hundred miles in altitude. The same object was seen in Belgium and Holland. The torpedo appeared to be solid. "Nothing could be more unlike a meteor...and too fast for a cloud," the observers remarked.

In 1949 astronomer Clyde Tombaugh, who discovered the planet Pluto, signed a statement saying: "I happened to be looking at Zenith, admiring the beautiful transparent sky of stars, when suddenly I spied a geometrical group of faint, bluish-green rectangles of light.... The group moved south-southeasterly, the individual rectangles became foreshortened, their space of formation smaller, and the intensity duller.... I was too flabbergasted to count the number of rectangles of light or to note some other features I wondered about later. There was no sound. I have done thousands of hours of night watching, but never saw a sight so strange as this...." And in 1955 astronomer Frank Halstead watched a shiny blimp-shaped object from the window of a Union Pacific train near Las Vegas. Halstead estimated it was about eight hundred feet long. As it paced the train, a disc about one hundred feet wide suddenly appeared behind it.

In 1957 a group fishing near Ubatuba, Brazil, watched as a flying disk seemed about to splash into the ocean. At the last moment it turned and climbed skyward. Moments later it exploded into fiery fragments. Some pieces were recovered from shallow water. The fragments were sent to a lab for analysis. The lab report indicated that the fragments were magnesium purer than any that could be produced by earth technology at that time.

All of these reports may well be of unidentified flying objects, or UFOs. Such accounts run into the thousands and come from all parts of the globe.

They continue into the present and range from simple sightings to alleged abduction experiences.

This book looks at some of the best-documented encounters with UFOs and extraterrestrial beings, or ETs. It presents the evidence—and lets you decide.

1

UFOs in SPACE

ASTRONAUTS AND UNIDENTIFIED OBJECTS

From time to time U.S. astronauts have spoken about UFOs and have reportedly made sightings or taken photographs. Indeed, astronaut Scott Carpenter photographed unexplained bright objects as he traveled above earth in his *Aurora* spacecraft in 1962. And in 1965, matching mushroom-shaped UFOs appeared in two photos of earth taken by *Gemini* 7 astronauts Frank Borman and James Lovell. Such photos, released by the National Aeronautics and Space Administration (NASA), are routinely explained as reflections, common objects, or space debris, or they may simply be left unaccounted for.

Rumors have circulated that *Apollo 8* astronauts photographed a gigantic UFO near the moon's far surface that was gone during their next lunar orbit, and even that *Apollo 11* astronauts may have sighted UFOs

(Opposite)
Unexplained twin UFOs appeared in this photograph of earth taken by *Gemini* 7 astronauts Frank Borman and James Lovell in 1965.

5

either before or after their historic moon landing. Indeed, Maurice Chatelain, a designer of the *Apollo* spacecraft and former NASA communications chief, has openly stated that all *Apollo* and *Gemini* flights were monitored by extraterrestrial vehicles but that this information was discreetly silenced.

While such controversial claims have not been verified, in 1993 a Japanese astronomer actually videotaped the shadow of a huge object moving across the surface of the moon at the astonishing speed of about one hundred twenty-five miles per second. The footage was released on American television. Russian scientists speculated that this may have been the shadow of an immense extraterrestrial craft,

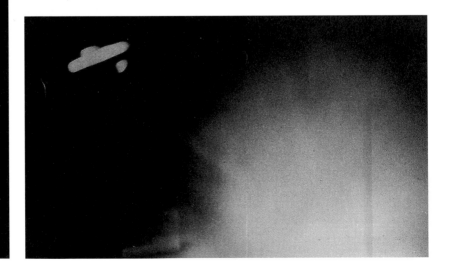

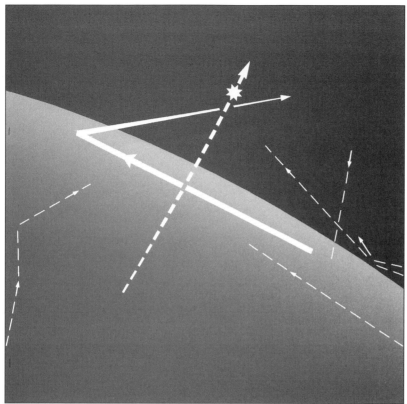

one able to maneuver easily around planets or other bodies in our solar system.

UFOs have also been observed and photographed from space shuttles orbiting earth. During a routine mission of *Discovery* in 1993, one of the astronauts videotaped the horizon, showing the bluish curve of earth with black sky above. The tape shows a prominent white dot moving parallel to the horizon against earth's silhouette. Suddenly the dot makes a sharp right-angle turn and accelerates into space. Within two seconds a light streaks upward from the ground, pass-

ing through the place where the white dot had been. The footage suggests that a missile was fired at a UFO, which defensively maneuvered away.

A NASA spokesperson explained the images as particles of ice from shuttle wastewater. However, Dr. Jack Kasher, a physicist from the University of Nebraska, traced the tracks of all the moving particles in the video. He concluded that there was no normal explanation for the movements of the dot, which not only turned a sharp corner in an instant but then increased in speed.

UFOS ON MARS

UFO reports have also come from the Russian space program. In 1989 the Russians sent a satellite to Mars. Named *Phobos II*, after one of Mars's tiny moons, it was to orbit just above the planet's surface. As *Phobos II* approached the Martian moon Phobos, it relayed photographs to earth. The last image showed a huge bar-shaped object next to the moon. Phobos is an irregular chunk of rock about seventeen miles long. The UFO next to it appeared to be almost as long as Phobos. Following this startling picture, no more photos were broadcast from *Phobos II*. The space probe became what the Russians called a spinner and simply disappeared for no apparent reason. One analyst suggests that the UFO was an asteroid photographed during the eight-second time exposure. Or it may have been a craft almost two miles wide crossing the open camera frame at around one hundred miles per hour. Some suggest that the

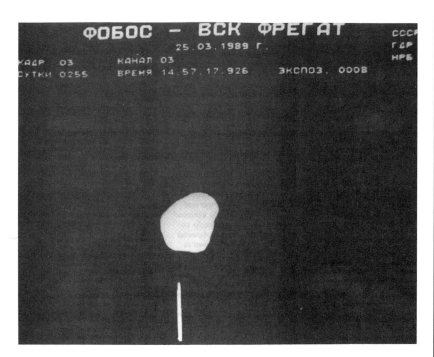

ФОБОС — ВСК ФРЕГАТ
25.03.1989 Г.
ХАДР 03   КАНАЛ 03
СУТКИ 0255   ВРЕМЯ 14.57.17.926   ЭКСПОЗ. 0008
СССР
ГДР
НРБ

UFO may have been an extraterrestrial mother ship that perhaps even kidnapped or destroyed the Russian satellite to avoid being monitored.

THE MARTIAN FACE

A U.S. space probe transmitted an equally puzzling image from Mars. In 1976 NASA launched a *Viking* orbiter to map the entire surface of the planet. It sent back images showing winding channels that looked like ancient riverbeds and sediment that looked like dried-up lakes and oceans. This led to speculation that in the very distant past Mars had a thicker atmosphere, rainfall, running water, and lakes and oceans similar to those of earth.

Most surprising, though, was that one set of *Viking* frames showed a huge "face" that seemed to gaze

skyward from the Martian surface. Although the computer image was grainy, the formation looked much like a huge human head, with eye sockets, a nose, and part of a mouth. There also seemed to be a helmet or headpiece that curved over the top and down at each side. However, one side of the feature was in deep shadow, so it could not be determined whether the "face" was truly symmetrical. The *Viking* image was published in many magazines. Some thought the "head" or "face" was the remains of a monolithic statue, like the great pyramids on earth—evidence that an intelligent race had once lived on Mars. But NASA officials stated that the "face" was an accident of light and shadow on regular surface features.

NASA announced no plans to analyze the image, and most people soon forgot about it. In 1980, however, image analysts Vincent DiPietro and Gregory Molenaar decided to examine the pictures further. Molenaar, who worked under contract to NASA, and DiPietro developed a computer process to enhance the details of the *Viking* images. This produced smoother and clearer pictures.

Several images of the "face" had been made in afternoon light coming from the west of Mars. One had been made in morning light coming from the east. This image was less clear, but it showed that the head was symmetrical, whatever the light, and was about one mile long. Image analyst Mark Carlotto took the process still further. Using a computer, he combined all available *Viking* images to produce a complete

(Opposite)
In 1976 a NASA *Viking* satellite image revealed a startling "face" one mile long on the surface of Mars.

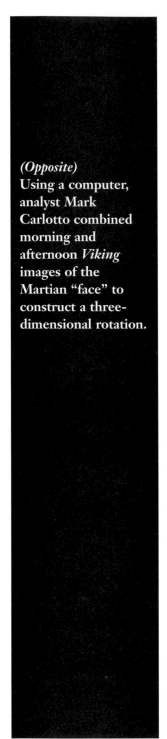

(Opposite)
Using a computer, analyst Mark Carlotto combined morning and afternoon *Viking* images of the Martian "face" to construct a three-dimensional rotation.

three-dimensional rotation of the huge head.

John Brandenburg, a physicist who also analyzed enhanced images, found several other formations that also resembled faces. One seems to have the same squared-off look of the first "face" and possibly a "helmet" or "headdress."

The *Viking* pictures reveal that Mars also has many pointed blocks that resemble pyramids. These are a common surface feature. Several located close to the original "face" are somewhat more regular, appearing to have four or five sides.

Could all these formations have been carved from natural features by an intelligent race, similar to the way the huge presidential faces of Mount Rushmore were produced on earth?

The mystery of the Martian "face" remains. The questions can be answered only when future cameras provide more detail, or perhaps when travelers from earth finally reach and explore the red planet.

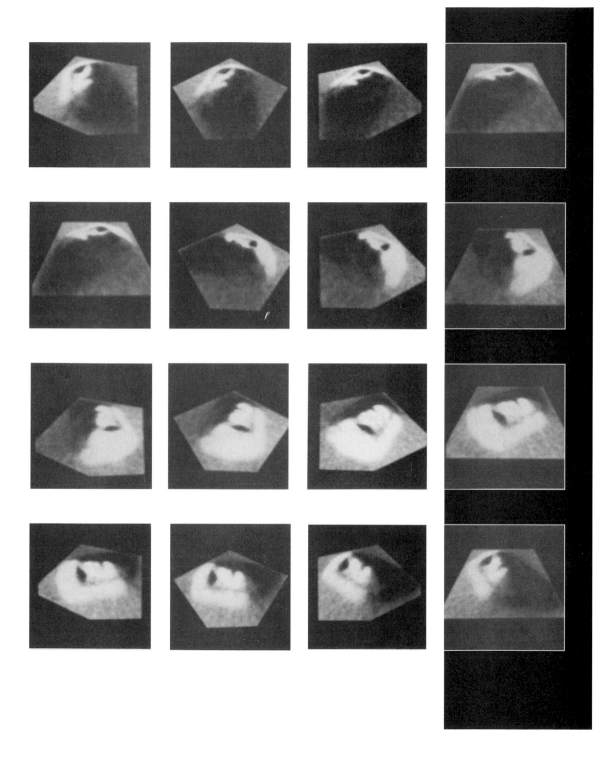

2

SIGHTINGS

UFO OVER PINEY WOODS

IT WAS THE NIGHT of December 29, 1980. Betty Cash was driving from New Caney to Dayton, Texas, through the Piney Woods. Riding with her were Vickie Landrum and Vickie's grandson, Colby. Suddenly a glowing object crossed above the pines and hovered over the road ahead at treetop level. The object was very large and was shaped like an upright diamond. At intervals red-orange flames shot downward with a whooshing noise, and there was a constant beeping sound.

Betty stopped the car to avoid driving under the craft. She had been using the car's heater, but it became so hot inside that all three stepped out into the December air. They could feel intense heat and heard a steady roaring sound from the object.

Colby became frightened, and he and his grand-mother went back into the car. Fascinated, Betty remained outside, gazing at the mysterious machine. By this time the sky had begun to fill with helicopters. Betty estimated there were twenty or more. Some had single rotors like the Huey helicopters from Tomball Airfield, northwest of Houston. Others were larger, with two rotors, like the Chinook copters from Ellington Air Force Base south of Houston. As Betty stared, the fiery diamond gradually rose and moved off toward the southwest, with the swarm of helicopters following.

When Betty returned to the car, the driver's door was so hot that she burned her hand on the handle. Once

A painting of the fiery diamond-shaped UFO, surrounded by helicopters, that Betty Cash and Vickie and Colby Landrum described seeing in the Piney Woods of Texas.

inside, she turned on the car air conditioner to reduce the oppressive heat.

By the time they arrived home, Betty, Vickie, and Colby were all ill. Betty had been outside the car the longest, and her symptoms were the worst. Her head and neck were blistered and had begun to swell. Soon her eyes were swollen shut. She became terribly nauseated. After four miserable days at home, Betty checked into a hospital, where she was treated as a burn victim for fifteen days.

Vickie and Colby Landrum had similar symptoms. Colby's face looked sunburned, and he, too, began to have problems with his eyes. He and his grandmother were nauseated, and where Vickie had rested a hand on top of the car, her fingernails had strange lines across them. Her scalp felt numb, and clumps of hair started to fall out. Some later grew back in, but with a strange, coarse texture. As time passed, all three continued to feel ill and tired.

Doctors listed their symptoms as life-threatening. These included skin sores, severe weight loss, and skin cancer. Some symptoms were similar to those of people who have experienced physical burns or exposure to nuclear radiation.

The "diamond of fire" encountered by Betty Cash and the Landrums had been seen by others that December night as it slowly crossed Piney Woods and descended over highway 1485. Yet when investigators checked with nearby air bases, none would admit to sending helicopters to the Piney Woods. And the blacktop road at the site, which apparently had been badly damaged by flames bursting from beneath the craft, was completely repaired in a surprisingly short time.

Investigators speculated that the mysterious aircraft was either an extraterrestrial vehicle or a secret experimental craft of the U.S. government or military.

Doctors verified that Betty, Vickie, and Colby had been badly injured. However, complaints to the military brought no result. The three filed for medical damages from the U.S. government and a congressional hearing was held, but the Department of the Army Inspector General issued a report denying any military or government involvement.

Whatever the identity of the mysterious and dangerous aircraft, it was—and is still—being kept secret.

LIGHTS IN RENDLESHAM FOREST

It was nearly midnight on December 26, 1980. In a rural section of eastern England, Gordon Levett was putting his dog in a shed for the night. He felt compelled to turn around and was astounded to see a large object hovering just over his cottage roof. It glowed white with a tinge of green and was shaped like an upside-down mushroom. Levett was transfixed, and his dog trembled in fear. The object drifted noiselessly, then slowly moved out of view.

That same night a target was picked up on radar at RAF Walton, an air force base about forty miles to the north. The unidentified object was moving at more than

nine hundred miles per hour. Two other stations, including London's Heathrow Airport, picked up the same radar target. It was headed toward Bentwaters Air Force Base, near England's North Sea coast. This was where Gordon Levett encountered the mysterious vehicle.

Several British RAF bases were leased by the United States Air Force and were part of NATO's European defense network. Bentwaters was one of these air bases; a short distance to the south was another, the Woodbridge NATO base.

On the night of December 26, Sergeant Jerry Stevens, a security policeman, and airman Joe Borman were standing guard duty at the Woodbridge back gate. They noticed the familiar blinking from the Orford lighthouse on the shore. But now the guards saw another light over the trees of Rendlesham Forest. It appeared to descend quickly into the woods. The men radioed their base. Two airmen, Jim Archer and John Cadbury, were immediately dispatched in a Jeep to check the woods for a plane crash or a fire.

The ground was rough, so the two men parked the Jeep before reaching the woods. As they approached, they saw lights through the trees. Arriving at a break in the trees, they observed a craft shaped like an astronaut's space capsule. It was about ten feet wide and eight feet high. It was round, with tubular "legs" angled out from the base, giving it a triangular appearance. The craft glowed with an eerie light that also illuminated the ground. A bank of red and bluish white lights ran across the middle.

Archer froze, but Cadbury walked toward the machine. As he reached out to touch it, his hair stood up as if it had received a strong charge of static electricity. The tubular legs retracted; the craft rose, moved back over the trees, and then maneuvered over a large grassy clearing. The airmen followed. Suddenly the

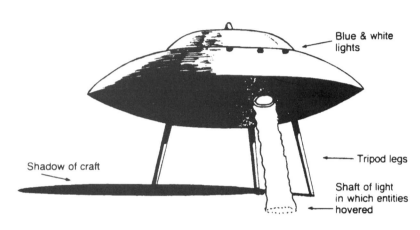

Blue & white lights

Shadow of craft

Tripod legs

Shaft of light in which entities hovered

A drawing of a craft that landed in England's Rendlesham Forest in December 1980. Tripod legs left radioactive depressions in the ground. Some witnesses perceived alien beings in a shaft of light.

vehicle shot upward rapidly. At the same time a radar operator at the base also watched a light rise from the forest and streak into the night sky. Personnel at Bentwaters also received reports of the sighting.

Early the next morning, base commander Colonel Ted Conrad took a team into the woods where Archer and Cadbury had sighted the unidentified craft. They found a break in the trees, damp ground, and three holes spaced in a perfect triangle about twelve feet across.

The next night began calmly. A new security team stood guard at the Woodbridge back gate. Then at around ten o'clock the team radioed the base to report lights in the direction of Rendlesham Forest once again, and a "firelike" glow coming from the trees. Another team was dispatched to meet the first at the gate.

In the woods the men saw a "curtain" of light in the pines, with a luminous mist rolling in underneath. There seemed to be an object with a red light on top and a bank of blue lights, much like what Archer and Cadbury had reported the night before. Once more, the UFO backed away.

Lieutenant Colonel Charles Halt, assistant base commander at nearby Bentwaters, brought a truck convoy of men to the woods just after midnight. The team carried portable spotlights, Geiger counters, star-lite scopes to view infrared light, and cameras. Colonel Halt used a tape recorder to make notes of the team's activities.

The path of Colonel Halt's truck convoy from Woodbridge Air Base to the UFO landing area in Rendlesham Forest.

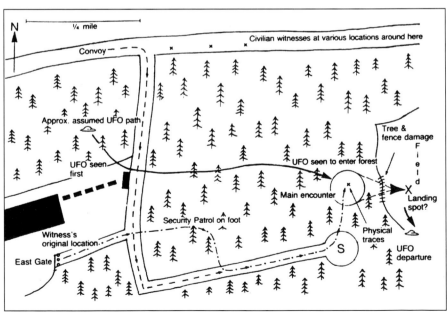

By the time the group arrived, the craft was gone. The men set up their equipment in the small clearing with the mysterious holes in the ground and, using the portable spotlights, studied the physical evidence.

A Geiger counter showed a slight increase in radiation at the site of the holes in the ground. In the middle, between the holes, the ground looked rough and scuffed. Radiation was much higher there, and the team labeled it the "blast point." Neighboring pine trees had horizontal gashes about four feet above the ground, all facing the triangular area. Some of the men thought that the craft might have bumped into the trees at that level. But the cut marks looked old, and sap was already oozing from them. The star-lite scope showed increased infrared, or heat, only from the sides of the trees facing the triangle and the "blast point." There were some freshly broken pine branches on the ground underneath the trees.

Four men were working several hundred yards from Colonel Halt's group. They were in a larger clearing near a farmhouse, checking the sky and woods for any strange lights. Gradually a glowing yellow-green fog formed in the clearing in front of them. One man later said it looked like a "transparent aspirin." It pulsed in an eerie way. Beyond the fog, a red light came toward the men from the woods, frightening farm and woodland animals away.

Simultaneously Colonel Halt's group spotted the red light approaching the clearing from their location in the woods. It pulsed on and off every few seconds. The

light was red on the top, and from underneath a "waterfall" of colors fell in a steady stream.

The multicolored light stopped directly in front of the four men in the clearing, hovering about five feet in the air. Suddenly the light exploded in a fantastic flash of sparks. Beneath the sparks there was now a craft poised just above the field. It had a rounded rim at the base and tapered upward into a dome. Glowing pieces continuously fell from it. Halt observed, "It...has a hollow center—a dark center—like the pupil of an eye winking. The flashes are so bright through the star-lite scope, it almost burns your eye." Halt continued, "Now we observe what appears to be a beam coming down toward the ground.... This is unreal." As the men watched, multiple light beams seemed to pass clear through the tree stumps beside them. Then, without warning, the craft rose, turned, and quickly and silently sped off into the distant sky.

Instantly the scene exploded in a flash of light later described as being as "bright as the sun." A blast of icy wind literally knocked out the men below. It was some time before most of them recovered, and one man did not regain consciousness for several hours.

The events at Rendlesham Forest are exceptional: They happened over a period of nights. There were radar trackings and radar tapes from nearby stations. There were observations by officers, airmen, and security police from both the Woodbridge and Bentwaters NATO bases, as well as by civilians. Broken tree limbs were found at the scene, along with impressions of

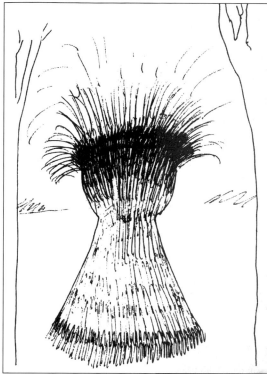

what may have been landing gear of a craft in the woods. And there were unusually high radioactivity and heat radiation readings at the site. Colonel Halt was later asked to prepare a summary of the case for air force files. This one-page report, secured through the British Ministry of Defense and the U.S. Air Force, was to become an important document to researchers.

A copy of Colonel Halt's tape also eventually became available to UFO researchers. It is apparently authentic but incomplete.

In 1991 British author Jenny Randles collected information for a book about the case called *From Out of the Blue.* In her account most witnesses described the UFO as a disk, though some refer to a triangular shape.

Two drawings of the UFO "light explosion" that took place in a clearing of Rendlesham Forest: *(left)* the sunlike light and shower of sparks described by Colonel Halt; *(right)* a sketch based on John Cadbury's impression.

REPLY TO
ATTN OF.   CD   13 Jan 81

SUBJECT: Unexplained Lights

TO: RAF/CC

1. Early in the morning of 27 Dec 80 (approximately 0300L), two USAF
security police patrolmen saw unusual lights outside the back gate at
RAF Woodbridge. Thinking an aircraft might have crashed or been forced
down, they called for permission to go outside the gate to investigate.
The on-duty flight chief responded and allowed three patrolmen to proceed on foot. The individuals reported seeing a strange glowing object
in the forest. The object was described as being metalic in appearance
and triangular in shape, approximately two to three meters across the
base and approximately two meters high. It illuminated the entire forest
with a white light. The object itself had a pulsing red light on top and
a bank(s) of blue lights underneath. The object was hovering or on legs.
As the patrolmen approached the object, it maneuvered through the trees
and disappeared. At this time the animals on a nearby farm went into a
frenzy. The object was briefly sighted approximately an hour later near
the back gate.

2. The next day, three depressions 1 1/2" deep and 7" in diameter were
found where the object had been sighted on the ground. The following
night (29 Dec 80) the area was checked for radiation. Beta/gamma readings
of 0.1 milliroentgens were recorded with peak readings in the three depressions and near the center of the triangle formed by the depressions.
A nearby tree had moderate (.05-.07) readings on the side of the tree
toward the depressions.

3. Later in the night a red sun-like light was seen through the trees.
It moved about and pulsed. At one point it appeared to throw off glowing
particles and then broke into five separate white objects and then disappeared. Immediately thereafter, three star-like objects were noticed
in the sky, two objects to the north and one to the south, all of which
were about 10° off the horizon. The objects moved rapidly in sharp angular
movements and displayed red, green and blue lights. The objects to the
north appeared to be elliptical through an 8-12 power lens. They then
turned to full circles. The objects to the north remained in the sky for
an hour or more. The object to the south was visible for two or three
hours and beamed down a stream of light from time to time. Numerous individuals, including the undersigned, witnessed the activities in paragraphs
2 and 3.

CHARLES I. HALT, Lt Col, USAF
Deputy Base Commander

Evidently it had both characteristics, and airman John Cadbury made a sketch combining these features. Airman Larry Warren described it as having intricate patterns on the surface and little "wings" that projected down at the sides. Though there was no outside source of light, he recalled: "As we walked around it we cast a shadow onto the side.... Every so often we would stop and our shadow[s] would take another step.... We did this three or four times." Somehow the reality of the observers seemed "out of phase" with that of the craft.

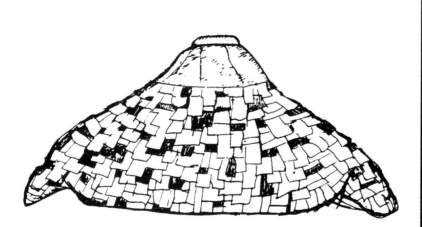

British Forestry Commission officers visited the site after the military had finished its investigation. A forestry plan had scheduled some of Rendlesham Forest for cutting. When the officers checked the woods, they said that the marks on the trees were old indications of which ones were to be felled. Strangely, although the "landing site" was not scheduled to be cut next, the day after the forestry officials' visit the area was stripped of trees.

A complete solution to the mystery of the lights and aircraft in Rendlesham Forest may never be found. But the case is important because it involves NATO military bases and the phenomenon of extraterrestrial landings or observations. Plus, there are more eyewitnesses and evidence present than for most UFO cases in recent years.

UFO FLAP IN BELGIUM

One of the most thoroughly studied UFO cases began in Belgium on November 29, 1989. That night thirty separate groups of witnesses and three police patrols all reported a large object flying at low altitude. The craft was flat and triangular, with lights underneath, near the rounded corners. It made no sound and created no air turbulence. Its movements were tracked from town to town across the Belgian countryside as it moved slowly between the town of Liege and the border of Belgium with Germany and the Netherlands.

Over the next few months many more reports came in. Twice, two F-16 fighter planes chased a mysterious UFO, but without results. On March 30 a call came in to military headquarters from a captain of the Belgian national police. At about the same time, two ground radar stations reported an unidentified target on their screens. One installation was a NATO base near Glons, southeast of Brussels. Glons contacted other ground radar and learned that a total of four military and civilian sites all had the same object on target. It was traveling slowly but failed to send the usual transponder signal to identify itself.

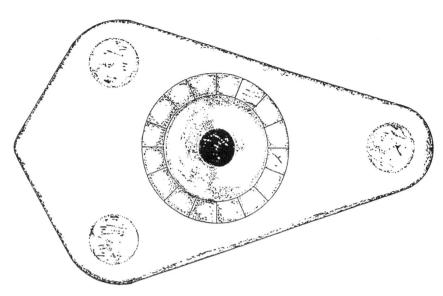

A sketch of a triangular craft seen over Mazy, Belgium, in December 1989.

Again, two F-16 fighters took to the air in the direction of the intruder. The F-16 radar spotted it, and the computer locked on to the target. As with all targets, it now appeared as a small diamond on the screen, and the computer tracked it automatically.

After five seconds, the target picked up speed and darted out of radar range. During the next hour, the UFO was locked on to the F-16 radar two more times as it played hide-and-seek with the planes. Finally the fighter's radar automatically locked on to the target at an altitude of seven thousand feet. In a few seconds it climbed to ten thousand feet. Within five seconds it dropped to only five hundred feet. Then, it disappeared below the range of both the F-16 and the ground radar, and both pilots lost sight of it in the maze of lights from the suburbs of Brussels.

Path of a UFO and an F-16 fighter giving chase over Belgium, both tracked by ground radar. The zigzag line of small dots is the F-16. The straight line of large dots is a UFO, which evaded the plane by making what were termed "impossible" changes in speed and altitude.

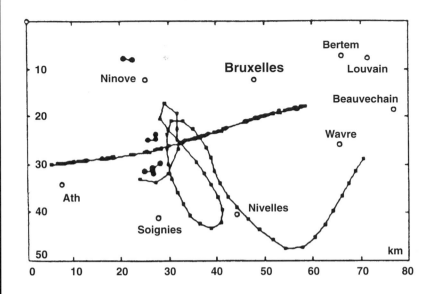

In dropping to five hundred feet, the craft must have traveled one and one-half times the speed of sound. But no sonic boom was heard. Such an altitude drop would create up to forty g's—and instantly kill a human. And the sharp turns at full speed that the vehicle made are impossible with present-day earth technology.

Sightings of a triangular UFO continued well into 1990. Altogether more than one thousand are on record. The dark triangular shape and colored "spotlights" were clearly visible to the naked eye both during the day and at night, and many observers tried to photograph the object. But photographers were disappointed to find that developed images were blurred and the craft outline was obscured. Professor Auguste Meessen, a physics teacher at the Catholic University of Louvain, puzzled over the problem. He guessed that infrared light might be the cause. In an experiment, he exposed some film to infrared. Then he photographed objects in ordinary light on the same film. Results were similar to the blurred UFO photos.

Nevertheless, a somewhat better image of the underside of a UFO was captured on videotape in April 1990. The "spotlights" were fairly clear, but the outline of the triangle was missing. When a still frame was enhanced by computer for contrast, the lights were

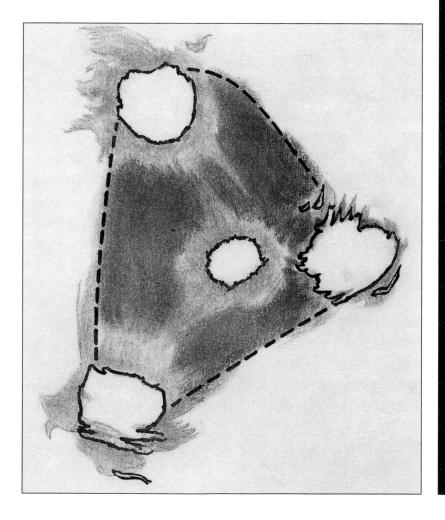

surrounded by brilliant streaks of red-orange, and the edges of the triangle now could be faintly seen. Sketches of the craft made by observers vary somewhat, but all show a flat triangular object.

Many have wondered why these sightings clustered in Belgium and did not spill over into the surrounding countries of France, Germany, and the Netherlands. One possible answer is that the Belgian highway system is so brightly lighted, it was visible even to the U.S. astronauts on the moon. No wonder otherworldly visitors might want to investigate Belgium.

The sightings in Belgium are remarkable for several reasons. First, there were well over one thousand reports. Second, observations came from the military, the national police, scientists, and private citizens. Third, civilian and military ground radar and military flight radar all tracked a UFO, and its flights were carefully charted and recorded on videotape. And fourth, all information was shared openly among the military branches, police, and civilian UFO researchers. This has never happened in any other country, including the United States.

CRASH AT ROSWELL

One of the most provocative UFO incidents dates back to 1947. Businessman and pilot Kenneth Arnold was searching for a missing plane in the Cascade Mountains of the state of Washington. He was surprised to see nine silvery objects flying at about nine thousand five hundred feet at a speed he estimated to be about one thousand seven hundred miles per hour. Arnold thought that the objects looked like boomerangs and later told a newspaper reporter that they flew like "saucers skipping across the surface of a lake." The reporter coined the term "flying saucer," a name that has been used ever since.

During the next two weeks, hundreds of crescent- or disk-shaped objects were reported in the West and Southwest, from Utah to Texas. And during the Fourth of July weekend, objects were seen in the skies around Portland, Oregon.

News accounts took an unusual turn on July 8, 1947, when a press release was issued by 1st Lieutenant Walter Haut from the air force base near Roswell, New Mexico. Thirty afternoon newspapers carried the story:

> The many rumors regarding flying disks became a reality yesterday when the intelligence office of the 509th Bomb Group of the Eighth Air Force, Roswell Army Field, was fortunate enough to gain possession of a disk through the cooperation of one of the local ranchers and the Sheriff's office of Chaves County. The flying object landed on a ranch near Roswell sometime last week. Not having phone facilities, the rancher stored the disk until such time as he was able to contact the Sheriff's office, who in turn notified Major Jesse Marcel of the 509th Bomb Group Intelligence office. Action was immediately taken and the disk was picked up at the

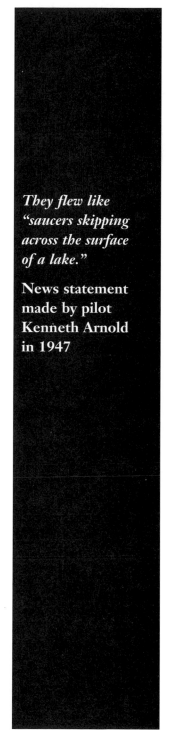

They flew like "saucers skipping across the surface of a lake."

News statement made by pilot Kenneth Arnold in 1947

Leased Wire
Associated Press

Roswell Daily Record

RECORD PHONES
Business Office 2288
News Department
2287

ROSWELL, NEW MEXICO, TUESDAY JULY 8 1947

5c PER COPY

Movies as Usual

Levees broke and flood waters rolled into the town of Grand Tower, Ill., but while the manager of this movie theatre swept out the water that has entered the lobby, movie youngsters are standing in line for tickets for the night's performance. (AP Wirephoto)

Claims Army Is Stacking Courts Martial

Indiana Senator Lays Protest Before Patterson

Washington, July 8 (AP)—Senator Jenner (R-Ind.) contended today that the high command of the European theatre is stacking courts against defendants in court martial.

In a letter to Secretary of War Patterson demanding a full investigation of army military trial procedure, Jenner offered what he said was documentary proof that

1. Prisoners are not being permitted to employ either civilian or military counsel of their own choice in the preparation and presentation of their defense.

2. Every effort is being made to prevent attorneys who were connected with the infamous Lichfield prison case to practice in courts martial in the European theatre.

The Indiana senator made public a copy of an informal "routine slip" which he said was signed by Brig. Gen. Cornelius E. Ryan, assistant deputy, military government headquarters for the military governor of Germany.

It was addressed to the chief of staff, USFET (presumably US forces, European theatre), was dated last Oct. 23.

It called attention to the impending arrival of Earl J. Carroll and Thomas Lester Poley, California attorneys, to act as special defense counsel for five prisoners then awaiting trial by general court martial at Frankfurt Aid Main.

Jenner identified Carroll as counsel in the court martial of Col. James A. Kilian in the Lichfield prison brutality case.

Carroll, then an army captain, resigned as assistant prosecutor in the Lichfield trials after asserting that a deliberate attempt was being made by army legal authorities to whitewash higher officers in the case. Kilian was later convicted and fined.

RAAF Captures Flying Saucer On Ranch in Roswell Region

House Passes Tax Slash by Large Margin

Defeat Amendment By Demos to Remove Many from Rolls

Washington, July 8 (AP)—The house passed today the Republican-backed bill to cut income taxes by $4,000,000,000 annually for 49,000,000 taxpayers, beginning Jan. 1.

It goes to the senate where approval also is forecast.

The vote was 302 to 11, or more than the two-thirds majority needed to override a presidential veto.

The action, which may encounter another presidential veto, came after Speaker Martin (R-Mass.) personally appeal to the house to pass the bill by such a decisive vote—as to persuade the president that the people should have this delayed justice.

The measure is identical with one vetoed by President Truman June 16 as the wrong kind of tax reduction at the wrong time—except that the effective date is changed from July 1, 1947 to Jan. 1, 1948.

Congress leaders expect to have the revised bill on Mr. Truman's desk before the week ends.

The house passed the bill after the Republicans beat back a proposed Democratic substitute that would have reduced taxes by $3,779,000,000 and removed 4,000,000 low-income persons from the tax rolls completely.

American League Wins All-Star Game

Chicago, July 8 (AP)—The American league, pecking away with an eight-hit attack and ringing the bell with its smashhitters, continued its all-star mastery over the National league by routing from behind for a 2-1 victory before a standing-room crowd of 41,123 at Wrigley Field today.

Woodburn Compares Farm Progress in Past Twenty Years

At Woodburn compared Chaves county agriculture with that of 20 years ago. In an address to the Kiwanis club today, crime that will fertility improvement processes have materially increased production.

As an instance he cited that 20 years ago lands in the county were yielding one-third sack of cotton per acre, whereas last year the yield was one and one-fourth sacks.

The communication ended with a request for assignment of some "alert and thoroughly competent lawyers" for the prosecution.

Jenner who served overseas as an air force captain, said the army marshal on courts martial specifically should be represented by civilian attorneys, or by any army officer of his choice. When none is requested, the unit commanding officer assume an officer to act as the legal counsel.

Cotton Acreage Is Above 1947 Figure

Washington, July 8 (AP)—The agriculture department reported today that the cotton acreage in cultivation on July 1 totaled 21,388,000 acres, or 17.3 per cent more than last year.

This year's acreage compared with 18,196,000 in cultivation a year ago and 24,817,000 acres for the ten-year July 1 average. The peak acreage was slightly more than 44,000,000 acres in 1926.

But the crop would be about 10,480,000 bales of 500 pounds gross weight if the acreage abandoned the 15-year average of 7.19 per cent and if the yield per acre is about the ten-year average of about 180 pounds.

The ten-year average acreage abandoned last year's acreage in cultivation on July 1 and the acreage in cultivation on the same date this year, respectively, by states indicated:

Texas 8,333,000 and 7,268,000. Oklahoma 1,176,000 and 1,130,000 and Arizona 3, 145,000 and 219,00.

Security Council Paves Way to Talks On Arms Reductions

Lake Success, July 8 (AP)—The United Nations security council today approved an American blueprint for arms reduction discussions despite a Russian warning that the plan would bring about a collapse of arms regulation efforts.

The vote was 9 to 0, with Russia and Poland abstaining.

In view of Russia's firm stand against the U. S. plan it had been believed she might provoke the fog power veto to block it.

Soviet Deputy Foreign Minister Andrei A. Gromyko gave his warning before the United Nations security council in a new effort to revise the Soviet working plan which already had been rejected by the commission for conventional armaments.

His challenge was taken up promptly by French delegate Alexandre Parodi and U. S. Representative Herschel V. Johnson, who abandoned their opposition to the American plan.

Gromyko insisted that his program for arms regulation could succeed unless the plan was linked directly with an absolute prohibition of atomic weapons.

He declared that the U. S. plan approved by the commission did not link the problems of arms reduction and the banning of atomic weapons and, for this reason, it offered no basis for a solution.

Gromyko opened debate on the arms question as delegates awaited another major declaration from him later in the day in reply to United States and British demands for action to restore order in the critical Balkan situation.

Delegates asserted they were approaching perhaps the gravest moment in U. N. history.

Gromyko said the U.S. program was not a plan he merely a document outlining a series of broad generalizations. The Soviet proposals on the other hand, he said, offered specific points which should be dealt with, such as the regulation of war production, distribution of armed forces and military transport.

"It is obviously," Gromyko added, "that the commission cannot work out a plan without linking it to atomic control."

No Details of Flying Disk Are Revealed

Roswell Hardware Man and Wife Report Disk Seen

The intelligence office of the 509th Bombardment group at Roswell Army Air Field announced at noon today, that the field has come into possession of a flying saucer.

According to information released by the department, over authority of Maj. J. A. Marcel, intelligence officer, the disk was recovered on a ranch in the Roswell vicinity, after an unidentified rancher had notified Sheriff Geo. Wilcox, here, that he had found the instrument on his premises.

Major Marcel and a detail from his department went to the ranch and recovered the disk, it was stated.

After the intelligence office here had inspected the instrument it was flown to "higher headquarters."

The intelligence office stated that no details of the saucer's construction or its appearance had been revealed.

Mr. and Mrs. Dan Wilmot apparently were the only persons in Roswell who have seen what they thought was a flying disk.

They were sitting on their porch at 105 South Penn. last Wednesday night at about ten minutes before ten o'clock when a large glowing object zoomed out of the sky from the southwest, going in a northwesterly direction at a high rate of speed.

Wilmot called Mrs. Wilmot's attention to it and both ran down into the yard to watch it. It was in sight less than a minute, perhaps 40 or 50 seconds, Wilmot estimated.

Wilmot said that it appeared to him to be about 1,500 feet high and going fast. He estimated between 400 and 500 miles per hour.

In appearance it looked oval in shape like two inverted saucers, faced mouth to mouth, or like two pie pans faced together with the soft billowish appearance.

The entire body glowed as though light were shining through from inside, though not like it would be if a light were merely underneath.

From where he stood Wilmot said that the object looked to be about 5 feet in size, and making allowance for the distance it was from town he figured that it must have been 15 or 20 feet in diameter, though this was just a guess.

Wilmot said that he heard no sound but that Mrs. Wilmot said she heard a swishing sound for a very short time.

The object came into view from the southeast and disappeared over the treetops in the general vicinity of six mile hill.

Wilmot, who is one of the most respected and reliable citizens in town, kept the story to himself hoping that someone else would see the thing and confirm his own before telling about what he had seen and what he had seen and about having it, this announcement that the RAAF was in possession of one came as a confirmation to the story that he had decided to release the details of what he had seen.

In view of their position, it appeared certain that a Soviet veto would provoke the worst crisis yet faced by the U. N.

Ex-King Carol Weds Mme. Lupescu

Former King Carol of Romania and Mme. Elena Lupescu relax aboard the S. S. America bound for Cuba and Mexico in May 1941. A member of Carol's household in Rio de Janeiro said the ex-king and the companion for 23 years in exile and exile were recently married at their hotel Copacabana Palace suite. (AP Wirephoto)

Miners and Operators Sign Highest Wage Pact in History

Washington, July 8 (AP)—An agreement averting a nationwide soft coal strike was signed today by John L. Lewis and a majority of the bituminous operators.

In announcing the signing Lewis told a news conference that it is "reasonable to expect" the entire industry will accept the agreement within a few days.

Washington, July 8 (AP)—An agreement under which 150,000 of the nation's soft coal miners will work virtually time and after at the highest wage in history was signed today.

Harry M. Moses, representing the steel companies, and Charles O'Neill of the northern commercial operators, signed for their operators employing the 150,000. Other operators from the Midwest and Far West who employ an additional 150,000 miners, were waiting their turn to put their signatures to the pact, negotiated by Moses and O'Neill on days of dickering.

The ceremony was held in Lewis offices at headquarters of his United Mine Workers.

Only the Southern group of operators producers of about 25 per cent of the nation's coal was left outside the ranks of those ready to meet Lewis' terms. Even they appeared willing to fall in line but

Air Force General Says Army Not Doing Experiments

Portland, Ore., July 8 (AP)—The Oregonian said today that Maj. Gen. Nathan F. Twining, chief of the Air Materiel command, told it flatly that the "flying saucers" are not the result of experiments by the armed services.

Washington, July 8 (AP)—The senate appropriations committee voted today to give the army air forces more than $10,614,419,799 for the current fiscal year, an increase of $251,424,219 over the amount voted by the house.

San Juan, July 8 (AP)—Bonds posted today all chance Yapolito's wife, primarily to force the United States government to abide by its agreement to move and appears free to proceed immediately with any job pending installation by the Balkan said.

Harrison said removal of the restrictions will strive many persons to proceed with their plans for business buildings and hotels which have been held up heretofore.

Two Oil and Gas Leases Are Filed

Two oil, gas and mineral leases were recorded at the office of County Clerk George Miller.

Fred H. Campbell to Selma E. Anderson, 80, section 15, T.15, R.25e.

Bulletins

Lake Success, July 8 (AP)—Russia today demanded United Nations action to put an end to "organized guerrilla warfare along the American aid to Greece until the U. N. supervision.

Washington, July 8 (AP)—The senate appropriations committee voted today to give the army air forces more than $10,614,419,799 for the current fiscal year.

Roswell Marriage Licenses

Marriage licenses issued at the office of county clerk Salvadora Chavez, 23, and Hermino V. Reyes 22, both of this city; Delbert F. Welch, 21, and Myrtle O. Evandine Reyes, 18, both of Roswell; Alvin A. Harp, 13, and Edna R. Patton, 43, both of Maladar; Texas; Marlin L. Berry, 18, and Joyce M. Mimbruoh, 19, both of Lake Arthur.

Held for Threatening Father in Law's Life

Bill Loy is held in the county jail until a hearing before Justice Marry Purcell on a charge of threatening the life of his father-in-law, Jim Bain, and hangs from all local and district complaints, it was reported.

Welcome to Roswell

QUICKIES By Ken Reynolds

Most commercially, grown orchids take five or seven years to grow from seed.

Some of Soviet Satellites May Attend Paris Meeting

Paris, July 8 (AP)—Indications mounted today that at least some of the nations within the Soviet orbit would attend the Paris conference on the Marshall aid talks.

A Sofia dispatch quoted an authoritative source as saying "probably Bulgaria will participate in the conference which opens in Paris Saturday." The dispatch said the Bulgarian council of ministers was meeting to reach a decision in the matter.

Roswellians Have Differing Opinions On Flying Saucers

Roswell is a bit uncertain about these flying disks, if would appear from inferviews today with a number of local citizens with about as many alike conceptions them as there are people interviewed.

Local Weather

Temperatures

Readings at 3 local interests from 2 p. m. yesterday to 11 a. m. today:

Dairymen of Area Hear Lecture Series

The first in a series of lectures on milk sanitation, sponsored by Chavez county dairy, was held at the Chamber of Commerce last night, and was well attended by dairymen from the Roswell area.

The lectures are supervised by J. R. Bliss, bacteriologist and instructor at NMMI Superintendent of the talks, as a means of disfurnishing the lecture area of milk borne disease among the area's dairymen.

rancher's home. It was inspected at the Roswell Army Air Field and subsequently loaned by Major Marcel to higher headquarters.

The press release was electrifying. The military had actually announced that flying saucers existed, and that one had landed!

Then on July 9 and 10, newspapers carried a new story released by Brigadier General Roger Ramey, commander of the Eighth Air Force, based in Fort Worth, Texas. According to Ramey, some wreckage had been found on a ranch, but when it was examined later at Roswell Field, it was claimed to be parts of a weather balloon.

Readers assumed that the first report was a mistake, and the public gradually lost interest. However, reports persisted, and this 1947 incident became one of the great cases in UFO history.

Over the years, several books referred to the Roswell case, including one written by retired Air Force Captain Kevin D. Randle and Donald R. Schmitt. It was entitled *The Truth about the UFO Crash at Roswell*. By the time this book was published, in 1994, almost two hundred and fifty people had been interviewed, including one hundred and twenty-five first- and secondhand witnesses.

According to Randle and Schmitt, the incident started late in the evening on July 4, 1947. During a rainstorm William "Mac" Brazel heard a crash louder than and different from thunder. The next morning he found wreckage scattered over a long strip in a field, as if

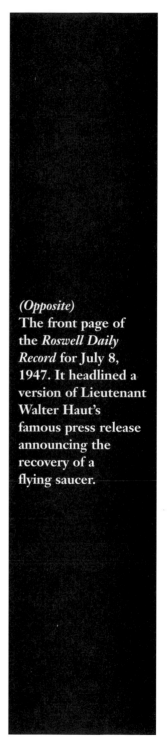

(Opposite)
The front page of the *Roswell Daily Record* for July 8, 1947. It headlined a version of Lieutenant Walter Haut's famous press release announcing the recovery of a flying saucer.

Leased Wire
Associated Press

RECORD PHONES
Business Office 2288
News Department
2287

Roswell Daily Record

VOL. 47 NUMBER 160   ESTABLISHED 1888   ROSWELL, NEW MEXICO, WEDNESDAY JULY 9, 1947   5c PER COPY

Gen. Ramey Empties Roswell Saucer

Lewis Pushes Advantage in New Contract

Southern Mines Only Hold-outs In New Contract

Washington, July 9 — The noble leatherneck today ...

U. S. Lend-Lease To Britain Looms As Needed by Fall

Decorated Veteran Records Discharge

Col. Fred G. Rowell, 103 South Kentucky, holder of the Italian Cross for Military Valor ...

Local Weather

Temperatures.

Sheriff Wilcox Takes Leading Role in Excitement Over Report 'Saucer' Found

35 Make Rotary's Century Club Roll

Attorney to Force Closing up of Ruidoso Clubrooms

Arrest 2,000 In Athens in Commie Plot

Revolution Was Set to Be Pulled Off Thursday

Athens, July 9 — The Greek government announced that more than 2,000 persons were arrested in the Athens area early today ...

Local Weatherman Believes Disks to Be Bureau Devices

Send First Roswell Wire Photos from Record Office

Pictured above are Jason Kellahin and R. A. Adair, of the Associated Press bureau in Albuquerque, as they sent out the first AP wirephotos ever to be dispatched from Roswell.

Romania Rejects Bid to Take Part in Economic Meet

Find Nude Body of Strangled Woman in New York Hotel

New York, July 9 — The nude body of a tall, blonde woman whose identity was not immediately learned was found today ...

Bulletin

London, July 9 — King George tonight announced the long-distance betrothal of Princess Elizabeth, 21-year-old heir to the British throne, to Lt. Philip Mountbatten, former prince of Greece and Denmark.

Ramey Says Excitement Is Not Justified

General Ramey Says Disk Is Weather Balloon

Tele n, July 9 — The flying saucer fever spread to Iran today.

Fort Worth, Texas, July 9 — An examination by the army revealed last night that mysterious objects found on a lonely New Mexico ranch was a harmless high-altitude weather balloon — not a grounded flying disk.

QUICKIES By Ken Reynolds

Welcome to Roswell

Harassed Rancher who Located 'Saucer' Sorry He Told About It

W. W. Brazel, 48, Lincoln county rancher living 30 miles north of Corona, today told his story of finding what the army at first described as a flying disk, but the publicity which attended his find caused him to add that if he ever found anything else short of a bomb he sure wasn't going to say anything about it.

Donate Freely to Aid Legion Juniors

something had exploded over a flight path from northwest to southeast. Most of the pieces were of a very strong, lightweight metal that Brazel did not recognize. The rancher took some pieces to show his neighbors, Floyd and Loretta Proctor. They were all surprised that the mysterious materials could not be scratched, dented, or even burned.

On Sunday, July 6, Mac Brazel drove to Roswell with a box of samples for Sheriff George Wilcox. Wilcox phoned Roswell Army Air Force Base. The phone call was followed up by intelligence officer Major Jesse Marcel. Colonel William Blanchard then dispatched Major Marcel and Captain Sheridan Cavitt, a counterintelligence agent, to the ranch, where the two worked all the next day collecting wreckage. The following morning more military personnel arrived to cordon off the area, and Mac Brazel was taken to the air force base.

When Brazel returned, he was detained by special military personnel. At the local newspaper, the *Roswell Daily Record*, Brazel now told a different story. Instead of the unusual materials, he said he had found pieces of burned rubber in a circle on the ground—part of a weather balloon of a type he had not recognized. Privately, Brazel revealed to his family that the wreckage was not a balloon, but the air force had sworn him to secrecy about the incident. Some witnesses believe Brazel was paid off by the air force.

In 1978, UFO researcher Len Stringfield interviewed Major Jesse Marcel. According to Marcel, most of the material he had gathered at the Brazel ranch was

(Opposite)
On July 9, 1947, the *Roswell Daily Record* announced General Ramey's explanation that the landed saucer was only a weather balloon. An accompanying article pictures Sheriff George Wilcox, a witness caught in the controversy.

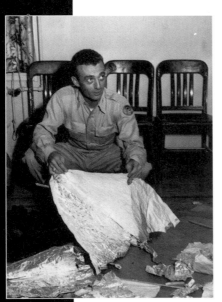

metal as thin as newspaper, but unbendable. Some pieces had flanged edges. Other materials he found were I beams that would flex slightly, tan material as light as balsa wood that would not break or burn, and strands of what looked to him like monofilament fishing line. (Decades later this material would be compared to modern fiberoptic filament.)

Although it was after midnight, Marcel stopped at his home on the way to Roswell to show his wife and son some of the wreckage he had collected. In May 1990 authors Randle and Schmitt learned more about this visit from Jesse Marcel, Jr.

During a specially arranged hypnosis session, Jesse Jr. recalled what happened that night in 1947. He was eleven years old and vividly remembered his father rousing him from sleep. He and his mother stared at the broken pieces laid out all over the kitchen floor. Jesse Jr. described a metal that looked like foil, a thicker metal that looked like Bakelite (a type of plastic), and strange I beams.

Under hypnosis he described unusual figures inscribed on one of the beams—"purple; strange; never saw anything like it...geometric shapes, leaves, circles"—and he also drew the symbols.

According to various reports, the wreckage collected at the Brazel ranch was driven to Roswell Air Field. From there it was sent to Fort Worth, Texas, where General Ramey issued his press release squelching the saucer story. By most accounts the debris was transported from Fort Worth to Washington, D.C., and finally from there to Wright Field and Patterson Air Force Base in Ohio.

In 1989 Randle and Schmitt interviewed Walter Haut, the air force officer who had issued the landed-saucer story. Haut disclosed that at that time Major Marcel had said of the wreckage: "It was something that he had never seen before and didn't believe it was of this planet.... I think there was one gigantic coverup on the thing. I think that somewhere all this material is stashed away."

As surprising as this information is, the account has a second part that is even more intriguing. On the same rainy Fourth of July that Mac Brazel heard the loud explosion, Jim Ragsdale and Trudy Truelove were camping in the woods perhaps thirty-five miles north to northwest of Roswell. Witnesses debated later over the exact location. Ragsdale saw a bright bluish light like that from an arc welder's torch. An object passed over the campsite and within seconds crashed about a mile away.

In the town of Roswell, two nuns making late rounds

"There were several bits of a metal-like substance: something on the order of tinfoil, except that this stuff wouldn't tear and was actually a bit darker than tinfoil in color— more like lead foil, except very thin and extremely lightweight. The odd thing about this foil was that you could wrinkle it and lay it back down and it immediately resumed its original shape. It was quite pliable, yet you couldn't crease or bend it like ordinary metal.... Dad once said it was not anything made by us."

Jesse Marcel, Jr. as quoted in *The Roswell Incident*, by Charles Berlitz and William Moore

37

at Saint Mary's Hospital, Mother Superior Mary Bernadette and Sister Capistrano, saw a very bright light fall to the ground in the northern sky. They thought it was an airplane crash and made an entry in the hospital logbook. They noted the time as between 11:00 and 11:30 P.M., July 4.

Archaeologists doing surveys of early Indian sites near Roswell also saw a bluish white object fall to earth. Because of the weather, they decided to wait until morning to search. And from fifteen miles southwest of Roswell Air Field, Corporal E. L. Pyles saw a glowing object that traveled across the night sky and then fell earthward. It had a halo and an orange glow. He was later not sure of the exact date, but Pyles remembered it was the Fourth of July weekend and near midnight, since he was up late after lights were out.

Jim Ragsdale and Trudy Truelove were closest to the site. Shortly after the crash they drove their Jeep across rough ground to the edge of a cliff. Moving farther on foot with a flashlight, they found a crashed airship but saw no activity. The flashlight batteries were weak, so they returned to camp for the night.

Investigators later learned that military personnel in the area were well aware of the crash. Three radar stations in southern New Mexico had been tracking an unidentified object in the skies since July 1. It had first been detected over the White Sands Proving Ground, where secret missile tests were conducted. During the evening of July 4, an unidentified radar target brightened and faded. Then it brightened again to a "sun-

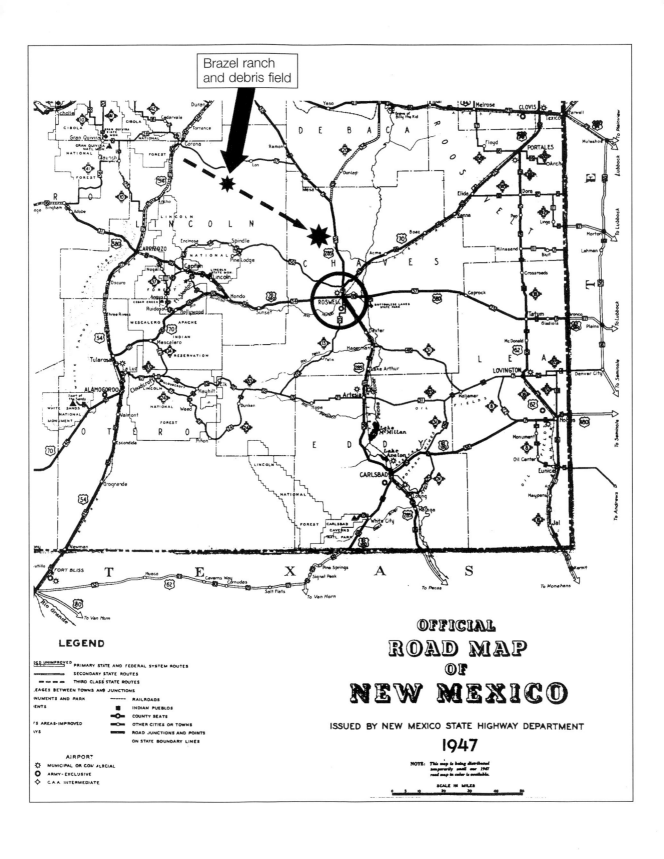

Brazel ranch
and debris field

burst" and disappeared entirely at 11:20 P.M. Technicians estimated that the impact area was north of Roswell.

The archaeology surveyors were among the first to arrive at the crash site the morning of July 5. One of them later described how they found a "crashed airplane without wings" and saw several small bodies on the ground nearby.

Jim Ragsdale and Trudy Truelove again drove the short distance to the crash that morning, only to find that the archaeologists were already there. Ragsdale later described a craft that had crumpled into the ground at an angle next to a cliff. He said there were several small bodies that looked like midgets outside the craft. According to Ragsdale, some of the scattered debris had unusual properties: "You could take that stuff and wad it up and it would straighten itself out."

Soon trucks bringing military police arrived, and the onlookers were ordered away.

Meanwhile a special team of investigators from Washington, D.C., had arrived at Roswell Air Field. Radar technician Steve MacKenzie, from one of the installations that had tracked the UFO, drove with them to the crash site. According to him, the craft had a hole torn in the side. There were five alien bodies: two outside the craft and three inside, one slumped in a small seat. Sergeant Thomas Gonzales from the Roswell 509th Bomb Group, who was one of the military guards, reported that the alien bodies were the size of little men, with heads and eyes slightly larger than those of adult humans.

(Opposite)
Two views of a possible UFO crash location north of Roswell: *(above)* **the recovery area from a distance, with the site at the base of the cliff toward the left;** *(below)* **investigators Tom Carey and Frank Kaufman stand near the base of the cliff where an extraterrestrial craft reportedly crashed with alien occupants in July 1947.**

Photographers from Washington had been included in the special team. They took photos at the site to record evidence outside and inside the wrecked craft. Shortly after, the bodies were placed on blocks of ice under a tarp in the back of a truck and transported to Roswell Air Field.

There, preliminary autopsies were performed on them at the army hospital. One hospital witness was Glenn Dennis, a young mortician in Roswell. He was telephoned that day by a mortuary officer from the army air base. The mortuary officer asked Dennis about baby caskets ranging from three feet, six inches to four feet in length and asked if they had an airtight seal. He also asked about how to preserve bodies so that their chemistry could still be studied later.

By coincidence, that day Dennis drove an accident victim to the base. As Dennis rushed into the hospital, two MPs forcefully escorted him back outside. The next day a base hospital nurse explained to Dennis what had happened. The bodies were those of aliens, and she had been present at the preliminary autopsies. The nurse later described the beings and drew sketches of them. According to her, the creatures were smaller than adult humans. Their hands had four fingers and no thumbs, and the upper arm bones were shorter than those of the lower arms. Their heads were larger than human heads, their eyes were somewhat enlarged and sunken, and their skulls appeared fragile. The nurse said the bodies reminded the pathologist of "ancient Chinese" people. They were partly damaged from the crash, exposure to

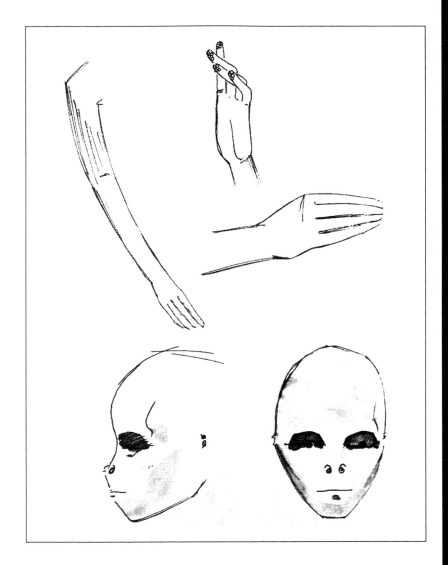

Drawings from sketches made by a nurse who assisted at an alien autopsy at Roswell Air Field in 1947. She described a humanoid with a large head and eyes, almost no nose and ears, forearms longer than upper arms, and tiny suction cups on the tips of four fingers.

the weather, and possibly from predators. The bodies gave off a toxic smell that made it hard to breathe.

Following the autopsies, the bodies were evidently quickly frozen and sealed into mortuary bags. The nurse and other Roswell personnel confirmed that the bags were sealed into a single crate that was placed in

an airplane hangar and was later flown to Fort Worth Army Base.

A key witness in the Roswell case was Norma Gardner, who worked at Wright Field, Ohio, in 1947. A civilian with a top-security clearance, she was assigned to catalog the events surrounding the Roswell case. Later Gardner revealed to family and friends that she had seen two of the bodies as they were being moved and had typed the autopsy reports that listed the beings as four to five feet tall, with large heads and slanted eyes.

Further support for the claim that alien bodies were recovered at Roswell came in 1995, when an alleged autopsy report dated July 14, 1947—more than a week after the crash—was made available by a civilian organization that investigates UFO reports. Originally marked TOP SECRET, the unsubstantiated document described a partly decomposed alien body that had arrived in a canvas bag. The being was thirty-six inches long and weighed only eight pounds. Its skin was a dark bluish gray. The nose consisted of two slits, and there were only holes in place of ears. The eyes were closed and almond-shaped. The cranium was large, and there was no jaw joint. The arms and wrists were very thin and long. The hands had only three fingers joined directly to the wrists. The body gave off a foul odor.

According to the autopsy report, a small mouth opening did not lead to a stomach. There were nonhuman internal organs but no lungs and no digestive system. Twin hearts were connected to three different types of circulation. The pathologist wrote that waste from one of these systems evidently could be eliminated through the skin. Bones looked like blue-green cartilage. A greenish liquid taken from the body was analyzed under a microscope and found to contain chlorophyll, like that found in earth's plant life. The pathologist wrote: "It is possible that photosynthesis was the means of obtaining energy.... This is not a cadaver of a kind previously observed by or known to this pathologist. It appears to be a form of creature utilizing elements of both the animal and the vegetable."

Researcher Len Stringfield received possibly related information from a doctor who reportedly performed an alien autopsy in the 1950s. Details included a lack of teeth, scaly skin that looked meshlike under the microscope, and feet that were covered with skin like a sock.

Still another alleged alien autopsy came to public attention in 1995. British filmmaker Ray Santilli was producing a documentary on rock-and-roll music. An elderly American photographer had kept movie footage of some rock musicians of the 1950s. The photographer also offered to show Santilli some other archival footage.

According to the photographer, he had worked under a military security clearance in 1947. In June of that year he was called to a desert area near White Sands Proving Ground, in New Mexico. He described seeing a crashed disk with several alien bodies, and one alien still alive. He first shot footage at the site and later was sent to Fort Worth Army Base to film an autopsy of one of the bodies. According to the photographer, most of the developed film had been sent to Washington, D.C. But several canisters processed later were still in his film collection.

Santilli was astounded at the autopsy footage and at first thought it must be a hoax. However, the grainy black-and-white film had code marks that dated it to the year 1947. And in the film the crude camera focus, as well as the clock, telephone, and surgical equipment that were seen in the examining room, were typical of that era.

The Fox network produced a documentary called "Alien Autopsy: Fact or Fiction?" that aired on TV in August 1995. It showed a humanoid about four and a half feet tall being examined by pathologists wearing protective clothing and head-gear. The being had a hairless head with a cranium larger than a typical human's and hands and feet with six fingers and toes. The abdomen was large. Muscles were similar to those of humans, but structure and proportions were different. The eye sockets and eyeballs were exceptionally large. The nose was very narrow and flat, and the small ears were set lower than on a human head. The narrow mouth was partly open and

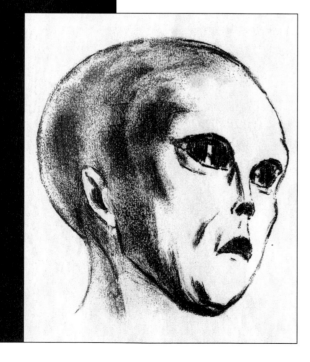

had almost no lips. Inside, there were no lungs, heart, stomach, and liver to be seen. Instead, a thick tube descended to a strange circular organ. A British forensic pathologist stated that the being did not look like a member of the human race as we know it.

The archival film seemed to partly support the Roswell case. However, no Roswell witnesses had ever reported a being with six fingers, and the Roswell incidents took place in early July—a month later than the alleged alien autopsy. And the White Sands missile testing site was west of Roswell rather than to the north or northwest. Are some witnesses wrong and others right? Are memories confused? Or is it possible that there was heavy UFO activity in New Mexico during the summer of 1947 and that there was more than one crash site with the recovery of differing alien bodies?

Even today Roswell is in the news. Through six months of 1994, residents Jose Escamillo and his brother Manuel claim to have used home video cameras to tape the flights of UFOs in broad daylight. A variety of UFOs were captured on the video, which was

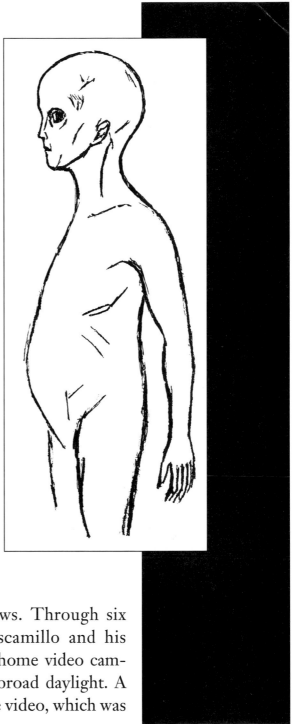

shown on the TV series "Hard Copy" in September 1994. Some are in silhouette; others are whitish or have a metallic cast. In one sequence a dark shape resembling a helicopter transforms into a bright disk as it moves through the air. Some video footage contains multiple UFOs that appear and disappear in a chaotic jumble across the daylight sky.

Also in 1994, the U.S. Air Force surprisingly issued a twenty-five-page document on Roswell. The document stated that the 1947 wreckage was a top-secret Mogul balloon designed to detect atomic explosions through sound waves trapped between the stratosphere and troposphere. UFO researcher Karl Pflock, working through the Fund for UFO Research in Washington, D.C., suggests that the crashed Mogul may be what was found on Mac Brazel's ranch. The balloon carried a radar target made of coated hardened balsa wood sticks and linen coated with foil, which might account for at least some of the witnesses' descriptions of strange materials.

However, it is doubtful that Moguls were launched during the time period when the wreckage was discovered. And of course the Mogul balloon story does not explain the eyewitness accounts of the second crash site north or northwest of Roswell, the details of the alien bodies shipped to Forth Worth and Wright Field, or the autopsy film footage discovered by Ray Santilli. Many UFO buffs believe that the air force document is simply another attempt to cover up some of the real events—nearly fifty years after the fact.

The Roswell case has many contradictions, and there are probably false claims. For example, author Donald Schmitt has been accused of misrepresenting his educational credentials, throwing doubt on earlier information, and creating conflict among investigators. But the number of witnesses who have come forward is now overwhelming. Even so, a full answer will come only if government and military agencies finally release the evidence that is still being withheld.

3

ABDUCTIONS

BARNEY AND BETTY HILL

ONE OF THE FIRST well-documented UFO abduction cases occurred in 1961. It involved a married couple, Barney and Betty Hill, who lived in Portsmouth, New Hampshire. They were driving home from a vacation in Canada, traveling south through the White Mountains. The night sky was clear, and Betty noticed a bright star that seemed to pace their car. The light became brighter, and finally the Hills stopped to look at it. By this time it resembled a large pancake hovering over the trees. Using Barney's binoculars, Betty saw a large craft with horizontal rows of windows. It made no sound. Barney then took the binoculars and crossed a field toward the craft. Through the binoculars he could see perhaps five figures in dark uniforms looking at him from the windows.

Frightened, Barney ran back to the car, and he and Betty continued driving down the highway. Then they noticed beeping sounds that they later described as being like someone "dropping tuning forks." They both felt tingly and sleepy. Confused and dissociated, they suddenly found themselves about thirty-five miles farther south, with no idea what had happened during the time it had taken them to travel the intervening miles. When the couple finally reached home, clocks showed that they had lost about two hours of travel time.

Betty's clothing felt odd, and she never wore it again. Barney's shoes were scuffed on the toes, as if they had been dragged over the ground. His body felt clammy, and several weeks later a rash developed around his lower abdomen. There were shiny spots on the car trunk, and a compass needle swung wildly when it was placed over one of them.

The Hills reported the encounter to officials at Pease Air Force Base, where the unidentified craft had actually been detected by military radar. Those who interviewed them said that the couple seemed sincere, but there was no logical explanation for their experience.

Two years later Barney and Betty met with Benjamin

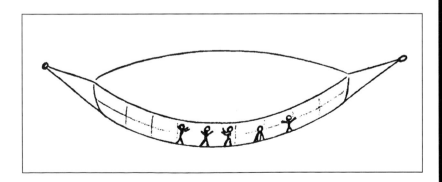

Drawing of the extraterrestrial craft observed by Barney Hill through binoculars.

Simon, a Boston psychiatrist, to resolve psychological and medical problems. Betty had been plagued by nightmares about being abducted by a flying saucer. And Barney had become disabled by health problems since their strange encounter.

Dr. Simon hypnotized the Hills separately and tape-recorded the sessions. He gave each of them a posthypnotic suggestion not to remember anything of the sessions. Barney and Betty told remarkably similar stories. Their car had been stopped at a roadblock after the beeping sounds occurred. They were taken aboard the flying craft and given physical examinations in separate rooms. They observed beings that looked somewhat human but, according to Barney, had large, upwardly slanted eyes that wrapped partly around their heads. The creatures had no true noses, and their mouths appeared to consist of narrow slits without lips.

Two sketches of the alien "leader" made by abductee Barney Hill.

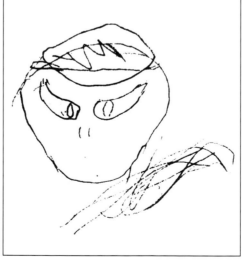 

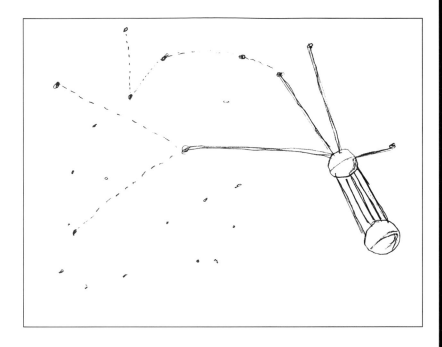

Sketch of a star map seen by abductee Betty Hill aboard an extraterrestrial craft. Large globes represent the double-star system known as Zeta Reticuli 1 and 2. Solid lines represent trade routes; dotted lines represent exploration routes. The stars closely match a three-dimensional model of the heavens.

The beings did not speak with their mouths but were somehow directly understood by Barney and Betty. Betty's impression was that they "talked" with an accent.

The aliens seemed puzzled about some of the differences between Barney and Betty: Barney was black, Betty Caucasian; Betty had her real teeth, Barney wore dentures. Each received medical procedures. A narrow needle was pushed into Betty's abdomen through her navel. She was "told" by the alien leader that this was a pregnancy test. After the examinations, the aliens instructed both Barney and Betty to remember nothing of what had happened. Only Dr. Simon's hypnosis sessions unlocked the traumatic memories.

In the early 1960s the Barney and Betty Hill case seemed one of a kind. However, medical details were reported in many later abduction cases. Often fluid samples were taken, including sperm samples from male abductees. And the "needle" examination of Betty was reported by other females. In 1961 doctors did not use a needle for such a purpose. Today, though, surgeons use a laparoscope, a long narrow optical instrument inserted through the abdominal wall to illuminate the inside of the body and transfer an image to a screen.

ABDUCTION AT BUFF LEDGE

Seven years after the Hills' experience, another abduction case occurred in New England. On a clear August afternoon in 1968 two counselors relaxed on a boat dock at the Buff Ledge camp in Vermont. Buff Ledge was a girls' camp located north of Burlington on huge Lake Champlain. The swim team had traveled to Burlington to compete in a meet that day, and the camp was almost deserted.

One of the counselors was Michael Lapp, a sixteen-year-old whose job was to maintain dock equipment and to ferry waterskiers to a raft in the lake. The other counselor was Janet Cornell, a nineteen-year-old water-skiing instructor.

The two counselors were watching the sun set over the water when they saw a bright light that Michael thought was the planet Venus. It suddenly swooped downward and closer, taking the shape of an elongated cigar. Michael shouted, "Wow! Venus is falling!"

As they watched, three smaller lights dropped from beneath the object. Immediately the large one swooped upward and disappeared. The three smaller UFOs then maneuvered above the lake. They stopped and started, made zigzags and loops, and descended like falling leaves. Gradually the crafts came closer to Michael and Janet. The UFOs moved into a triangular formation, and then two of them departed in different directions, making sounds Michael remembered as being like "thousands of different tuning forks."

The third UFO passed, then shot upward and disappeared. It reappeared immediately, tilted to one side, and dropped into the lake. In a few minutes it emerged from the water and glided toward the dock. Through a transparent dome Michael saw two childlike figures. Their heads were unusually large, greenish blue, and hairless. Their necks were long and thin. Large eyes extended beyond the sides of their heads, reminding Michael of a frog's eyes or of goggles.

A diagram of the path of a UFO approaching the boat dock and counselors at Buff Ledge camp in Vermont, made by investigator Walter Webb.

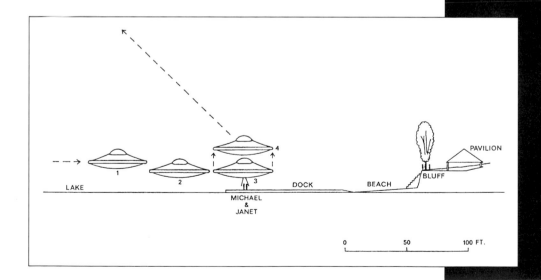

Michael sensed a telepathic communication with the small figures. Once he slapped his knee and laughed. At the same instant one of the figures in the window slapped a knee in imitation.

The craft moved overhead, and a cone of bright light shot downward. Michael grabbed Janet by the shoulders as they both fell to the dock. He thought they would be kidnapped and shouted, "We don't want to go!" Although he could look into the light without squinting, it was so bright that the bones in his hand stood out like an X ray. The light seemed to have a liquid quality, and Michael had the sensation of swirling and floating upward.

His next awareness was of looking up at the craft again from the dock. The sky was now dark, and he

Sketch of craft, dome, and small figures made by Buff Ledge camp worker Michael Lapp. Surface tiles resemble those observed on a disk that landed near Woodbridge, England, twelve years later.

wondered if he had been lying there unconscious. Janet was also lying on the dock, dazed and disoriented. Almost immediately the counselors heard the sounds of campers returning from the swim meet. The UFO then lifted higher, its light beam flashed repeatedly across the camp, and within a few seconds it had vanished into the night sky.

The next day Michael and Janet had no opportunity to talk about their experience, and in a few weeks the summer season ended and they went their separate ways.

Although Michael spoke little of his experience, about five years later he began to have vivid dreams of being on board the UFO. Finally, more than ten years after the encounter, he contacted the J. Allen Hynek Center for UFO Studies (CUFOS). CUFOS investigator Walter Webb suggested that Michael undergo hypnotic regression, and he agreed.

During hypnosis Michael recalled his experience with the UFO. He described how the cone of light lifted him on board the small craft, which then entered a mother ship. He reported watching Janet as she lay on a table. Small aliens looked into her eyes with a light as they used a screen with changing colors and lines, seemingly to monitor her. They also appeared to scrape her skin and withdraw fluids from her body.

Michael described the beings as all looking much alike. He said the head looked "like a bean on its side...like a lima bean," and it sat on a thin neck above sloping shoulders. The face had large oval eyes with round black irises surrounded by white areas, a mouth without lips, no ears, and two openings for a nose. The arms were thin, and the hands had three pointed and webbed fingers. Michael described the beings as shiny-looking with bodies that felt "wet" and "clammy."

According to Michael, the beings conveyed that they

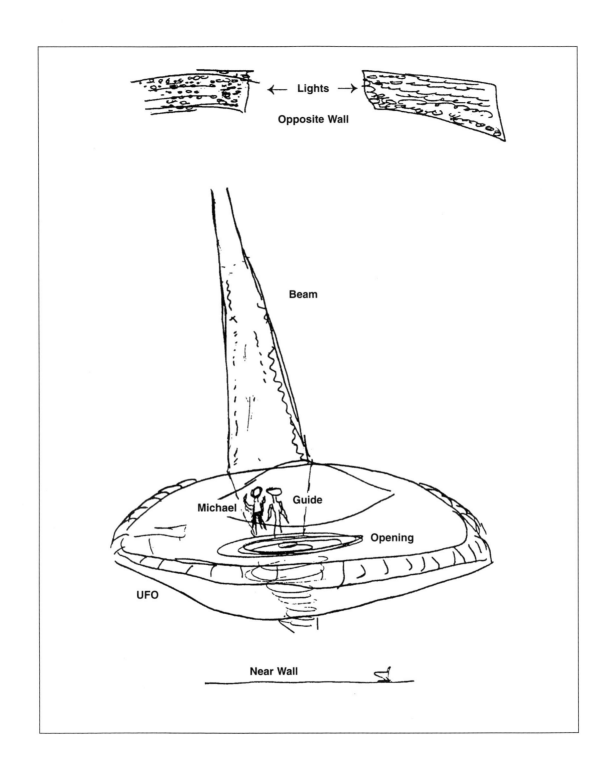

had been visiting earth for a long time. They were apparently concerned about the effects of atomic weapons. One of their purposes, Michael said, was to "make life like ours...other places."

When Janet underwent hypnosis, she described her abduction with similar details. She remembered being cold during an examination on a table and recalled something pinching her neck and pulling her hair.

Walter Webb later located others from the camp who confirmed seeing unusual lights at the dock the night the swim team returned. Two more counselors recounted a separate experience earlier in the summer, in which they watched lights maneuvering over Lake Champlain for about twenty minutes. As with Michael and Janet, one light approached the dock and hovered. Webb also learned that 1968 was a year with an unusual number of UFO humanoid reports, including several in the northeastern United States and Canada.

Although it was not investigated until ten years after the event, the Buff Ledge encounter is one of the most thoroughly studied abduction cases in recent years.

ABDUCTION ON THE ALLAGASH

A startling multiple-abduction case involves four young men. Twins Jim and Jack Weiner had met

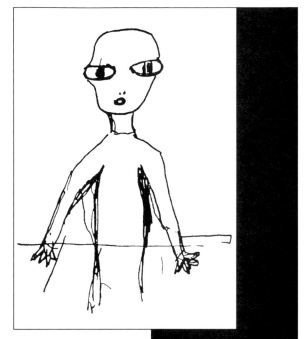

A sketch of an alien figure made by Michael Lapp, based on conscious memory.

(Opposite) Michael Lapp drew himself as an abductee in a small alien craft, which docked inside a huge mother ship. He felt himself floated along the tube-shaped beam.

Chuck Rak and Charlie Foltz at the Massachusetts College of Art, and all were beginning careers as commercial artists. In August 1976 they took a canoeing vacation together on the Allagash Waterway, a series of lakes and canals in the mountains of Maine. Midway through their trip they reached Eagle Lake, where they paddled to the mouth of a brook to fish. They had no luck, and their supply of fresh food was low, so they decided that night fishing would be worth a try.

After preparing a camp dinner they built a huge bonfire to mark their location. The four men then took their canoe out on the darkening lake to do some quiet fishing.

Suddenly they saw a light brighter than a star hovering over the trees. It reminded them of the fiery glow inside a pottery kiln. With a gyroscopic motion it changed from red to green, then to whitish yellow. It made no sound, and the men estimated it was two hundred or three hundred yards away and perhaps eighty feet in diameter.

As the object drifted above the shoreline, Charlie Foltz signaled an SOS with his flashlight. Immediately the UFO moved silently toward the canoe. As the men paddled desperately for shore and their campfire, the object sent a hollow cone-shaped beam downward toward the canoe.

The next thing the men knew, they were standing on the shore. Charlie Foltz aimed the flashlight at the object once more, but it rose with a stair-step pattern, flashing its own beam of light through small clouds. It "winked out," Foltz later recalled, then reappeared and

finally "winked out" once more among the stars. The men found to their amazement that their huge campfire had burned down to nothing but coals. This should have taken two or three hours, but the men could not account for the missing time.

Two years after the experience on the Allagash Waterway, Jack Weiner began having nightmares. In them, beings with thin necks and large heads examined one of his arms while Jim, Chuck, and Charlie sat on a bench, unable to help. The beings had large metallic and phosphorescent eyes with no lids, and their hands were insectlike, with only four fingers.

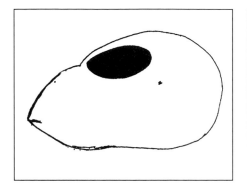

Alien faces "like bugs," sketched by Jim Weiner, one of four young artists abducted from a canoe on the Allagash Waterway in Maine.

The other three members of the canoeing expedition also had similar abduction dreams and flashes of memory. Finally, in 1988, Jim Weiner attended a UFO conference where he met author and UFO researcher Raymond Fowler. Fowler felt that it was unusual to find four firsthand-encounter witnesses. He suggested that the men undergo separate hypnosis to try to recover more memories.

Their hypnotic recall suggested that all four had been abducted into the large craft from the canoe by means of the strange beam of light, much as had apparently happened to the waterfront counselors at Buff Ledge camp eight years earlier. The men all remembered uncomfortable physical examinations involving skin scrapings and fluid samples. These were similar to those described in both the Buff Ledge case and the case of Barney and Betty Hill, but with different details of procedures and technical equipment.

The men's descriptions of the aliens were vivid. Each noted elements that stood out in his own experience.

Because the men were all trained artists, they made many sketches of their abductors, the craft, and the examination devices. Jim Weiner described the aliens as thin, with exoskeletons like those of bugs and with "connected fingers." They wore bluish gray clothing somewhat like ski suits. Jack Weiner said the beings' heads looked "like eggs.... They've large eyes on the side of their heads. There's no nose...and their mouths are on the bottom, like turtle mouths." According to Jack, their "joints don't move right." He described four same-size fingers and no thumb. Jack made detailed drawings of the aliens' hands. They were clawlike, with a split so that

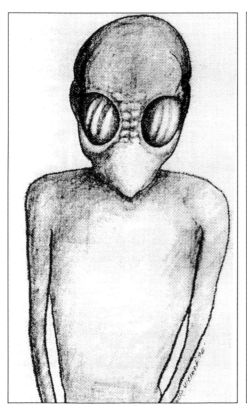 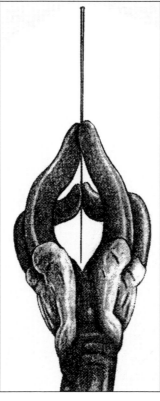

Drawings by Allagash artist and abductee Jack Weiner: *(left)* a front view, showing unusual texture on an alien head and a "turtle-like" mouth; *(right)* Jack Weiner drew the remembered detail of an alien hand, with pairs of opposing fingers.

the two pairs of fingers closed together. He described the aliens' feet as having the same split between two parts.

Charlie Foltz also drew the beings, describing their heads as almond-shaped with large "Asian almond eyes." He said that the eyes blinked like a bird's, with a flash that "goes across the eye." According to Charlie, the noses were flat and the ears did not protrude. When he was asked if the aliens had mouths, he answered, "They don't have...like a mouth...like if your lips were sealed."

Under hypnosis, Chuck Rak said the alien examining area had a silvery table and "looks like the vet's office."

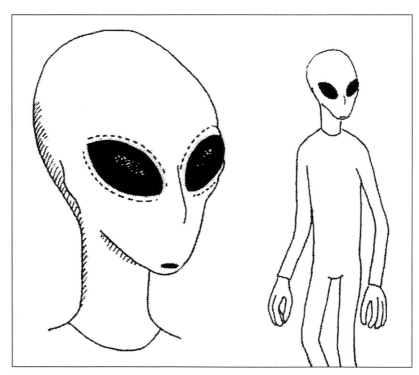

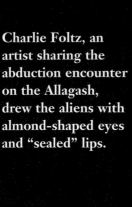

Charlie Foltz, an artist sharing the abduction encounter on the Allagash, drew the aliens with almond-shaped eyes and "sealed" lips.

He related difficulty in focusing on the alien examiners: "Don't have a very clear image of them—they're not the same—not the same frequency. It's like a radio station—can't get it tuned in clear."

According to Rak, the alien head was oblong from front to back, like an "embryonic chicken head." The neck looked like a "turkey gizzard," and there were embryonic folds under the eyes. Under psychiatric examination, all four men were judged to be in normal mental health, and each successfully passed a lie-detector test.

Taken together, the hypnosis tapes and drawings of the four professional artists provide strong evidence for the reality of their abduction experience on the Allagash Waterway.

"INTRUDERS" IN INDIANA

During the next two decades many more abductions were reported and studied. One case involves a woman from Indianapolis who had experiences throughout her life.

Debbie Jordan had made plans to visit a friend, whom we will call Dee Ann, the evening of June 30, 1983. Just before 9:00 P.M. she glanced out the window of her house, which she shared with her son and her mother, Mary. She saw an unusual whitish light in the backyard poolhouse. The poolhouse door was open, but Debbie had just been outside and knew that the door had been closed. As she pulled out of the driveway a few minutes later, she noticed that the garage door, which had been shut, was now open. When Debbie arrived at her friend's house, she called home to check

on Mary, who said everything was all right. Shortly afterward, Mary looked out the back window and saw a ball of light surrounding the birdhouse.

Mary picked up the phone again to ask Debbie to return home. Debbie arrived at about 9:30. She took out her father's rifle and carried it into the backyard. After what seemed to Debbie and her mother only about ten minutes, Debbie brought the gun back inside and said everything was fine. She then drove back to invite Dee Ann and her daughter, Tammy, for a swim. However, when Debbie reached Dee Ann's house it was actually after 11:00 P.M. Both Dee Ann and Tammy were surprised to see Debbie so late, but they agreed to go back to the Jordans' to swim. Nobody thought about it then, but over an hour of time was missing.

Walking toward the pool, Tammy cried, "Ouch!" as she stepped barefoot on a spot of hot, dry ground where she expected cool grass. Once in the pool, the three swimmers began to shiver, although the night was hot and the water was warm. All of them felt nauseated. Debbie had not put her head underwater, but her eyes started to burn and she later developed an eye infection.

The same evening at around 10:45 the Jordans' next-door neighbor, Joyce Lloyd, was cleaning house and watching TV. Suddenly she saw a flash of light from the vicinity of the Jordans' backyard. The Lloyd house shook. The TV blanked out in a red light, and the room lights dimmed. Joyce was sure there had been an earthquake. But Mary Jordan noticed nothing.

Within two days the Jordans were astounded to find

a circle of burned grass in the backyard where Tammy had stepped. A path of partly burned grass about two feet wide extended from the circle across the backyard for nearly fifty feet. The grass in the marked areas had died off. The soil was hard and dry and smelled pungent. Nearby trees began to wither. Debbie's father placed a Geiger counter over the dried circle to measure radiation. The needle instantly flipped to the maximum reading and stayed there.

Debbie had already contacted UFO author and researcher Budd Hopkins, and she mailed him samples of soil from inside the circle and from just outside the affected area. Hopkins sent the samples to a lab for

Circle and path of burned ground in the Jordans' backyard in Indiana, where an alien craft apparently landed in June 1983. Marked area showed radioactivity. Snow melted off of the area for two years, and it remained visible for over five years.

analysis. According to the lab's report, the unaffected soil contained normal signs of microscopic life. But the sample from the burned circle was dried out and more dense. It had lost 60 percent of its calcium and had no life whatsoever.

Debbie Jordan traveled to New York City to meet with Hopkins. There she underwent hypnosis to help her recall more details of her missing time the evening of June 30. She remembered standing in the garage doorway with the rifle, gazing at an egg-shaped craft on jointed legs in her backyard. A ball of light moved up and down as if "looking" at her. Debbie remembered that something pulled down on her right shoulder. Then her right ear felt as if it was being poked with a pencil. This same ear later became painfully infected.

Another of Debbie's experiences related to a vivid dream she had had in 1978. Before going to bed she'd had an ominous feeling and had left both the TV and the stereo on. Later, hypnosis uncovered a memory of being abducted and of receiving a physical exam. She recalled that two probing needles were placed into her nose, one in each nostril, and that a collar was fastened around her neck. She had looked up to see the huge black eyes of a gray-skinned creature peering down as if to reassure her. Debbie was then startled to awaken in her nightgown in the backyard. As she looked toward the sky, a UFO slowly moved away. When she returned to the house, the doors were locked, and she called to her mother to let her in. The TV and stereo were off. The next morning she found tiny bloodstains on the bed sheet just where she had "dreamed" the collar was fastened around her neck.

Debbie's impressions of a probe in the ear and in the nasal sinuses are similar to those of other so-called abductees. A few abductees describe a tiny object about the size of a single buckshot on the end of the needle or probe. Many later have nosebleeds, infections, or other discomfort, just as Debbie did. Researchers speculate that during these procedures tiny implants may be introduced into the central brain. Perhaps such implants allow an alien intelligence to track humans or in some way communicate with them. It may be much the way our scientists tag animals for identification. Abductee implants actually have been

(Left) **Debbie Jordan drew the type of alien being she encountered many times throughout her life;**
(right) **Debbie's sister, Kathy Mitchell, drew an alien "mantis" type she believes she had encountered.**

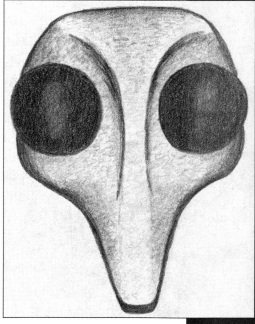

recovered from various parts of the body. Indeed, hospital videotapes show identical half-inch triangular objects, one from a toe and another from the back of a hand, that were surgically removed from two people who had never met.

After her implant experiences and shortly before she was to be married, Debbie Jordan discovered that she was expecting a baby. At first things went well, but within two months the fetus simply disappeared. Debbie and her doctor were mystified. However, through dreams and subsequent hypnosis, recovered memories suggested that Debbie's baby may have been abducted. Debbie believes she was later shown a young girl that was a daughter she had never known. The girl looked like a combination of a human and an alien being.

Only in recent years can we even imagine that such an experience may be factual. For instance, the surgical laparoscope can now remove an egg from the uterus to be fertilized outside the body and replaced in the mother's uterus to grow as a normal baby.

THE SALTER CASE

While some so-called abductees have frightening episodes, others report positive experiences. An example is the case of John Salter, Jr., which took place when he was a faculty member of the University of North Dakota. In March of 1988, he was headed for a speaking tour of the Deep South, traveling in a pickup truck with his son, John III. Without explanation John Jr. turned the truck off of Route 61. Over an hour later the two men found themselves headed in the wrong direction.

The following day they continued their drive south, puzzling over the "lost time." Suddenly a shining UFO with a silvery "energy field" appeared over the highway. John Jr. and his son both sensed a friendly and familiar feeling about the object. After that they had flashbacks, gradually recalling what had happened.

They remembered that their truck had been stopped that first night. John and his son stepped out as a group of small aliens came to examine the vehicle inside and out. John Jr. thought they looked like children. Soon a taller being appeared that looked part-alien and part-human. The group led the men away from the truck. On the path John Jr. stumbled but was prevented from falling by a strange force that he believed emanated from the beings. He felt protected by them.

John and his son were taken into a simple room with curved walls. Each lay on a chair like that in a dentist's office. The men felt immobilized as they were examined. John Jr. later described several procedures. First, an implant was painlessly placed up his right nostril "and beyond." Next something was injected into the side of his neck, and then another injection was made at the top of his chest. He associated the implant and these injections with three endocrine glands: the pituitary, at the base of the brain; the thyroid, in the neck; and the thymus, behind the breastbone. John Jr. knew that these glands helped regulate growth, metabolism,

and immunity. Following the procedures, he sensed a strong bond with the humanoids and a communication from them that they would all meet again later.

Following the abduction, John Salter Jr. noticed an improvement in his health. His hair grew faster and thicker, and his fingernails grew more rapidly. A scar on his forehead faded and almost completely disappeared. And one day he simply stopped smoking without even thinking about it. To the Salters, their abduction experience was an entirely positive one.

Many other abductees have also come to feel that there is a useful purpose to the experiences. Some find themselves with unusual psychic abilities or vastly improved intelligence levels. Some sense that alien intervention is preparing earth dwellers to work with all life in the universe.

ABDUCTOR TYPES

Many different alien forms are reported by abductees. They range from tall humanoid beings to tiny bald-headed creatures to those with reptilian characteristics. The most common type has been nicknamed the "grays." These are generally from three to five feet tall, with large heads, almond-shaped eyes, and fragile bodies. A second type, sometimes called the "mantis," has a head resembling a praying mantis. A third commonly reported form is a blend between a human and an alien. In the 1970s UFO investigator Raymond Fowler wrote about the case of Betty Andreasson, a Massachusetts housewife. Betty allegedly was taken aboard a craft where she saw tiny human fetuses nourished in containers of fluid. When she asked about the fate of these babies, she was told by the aliens, "They become like us."

Why would aliens wish to raise humans or interbreed with us? By some abductee accounts, an extraterrestrial species may be dying out. The beings are trying to prevent this by breeding hybrids between earthlings and themselves. Perhaps it is not so different from the way farmers breed better cows and horses, or strains of fruits and grains, that are healthier and more resistant to disease.

Two impressions of a "mantis" type of alien drawn by the author, based on personal recollection.

An alleged alien autopsy report dated July 14, 1947, described such a being as Betty Andreasson may have observed. It was forty-four inches long and weighed twenty-seven pounds. It looked like a human embryo that had been artificially matured, with a head that was large compared with the body. Hands, feet, skin, and nails were fully formed. Other organs had been completed with a kind of cosmetic surgery. Where ears and nose had not yet formed, skin had been stretched to form delicate-looking organs. The pathologist wrote: "Eyes...were almond-shaped and by far the most prominent facial feature. The eyeballs were not matured and appeared to have been sutured with artificial lenses of an unknown type."

Lungs were not developed. The stomach was not used, and the pathologist stated: "It is probable that this individual did not breathe any more than he ate. The means of sustaining life is unknown." The heart was large, and all circulation was filtered through the liver. The skull was very thin. The pathologist was amazed to find an extra section of brain over the usual layers and wrote: "The brain itself was extensively and surprisingly formed."

So many people have now reported abduction episodes that university researchers have begun to pay attention. A Roper Poll has reported that one out of every fifty people in the United States has had such an experience. Temple University history professor David Jacobs published a collection of abduction cases. MIT physics professor David Pritchard and John Mack, a psychiatrist from Harvard Medical School, organized an Abduction Study Conference dealing with individuals whose UFO experiences were not connected to known mental disturbances. And psychiatrists and psychologists have formed encounter groups in which so-called abductees can share the strangeness of their experiences and memories.

Some researchers feel that encounters with ETs are real physical events. Others believe that they may be more like dreams or inner realities constructed by the individual's subconscious mind. Or they may be inter-actions between differing realities. Whatever the source, abduction experiences have become the subject of serious study.

4

SOLVING THE UFO PUZZLE

MANY PROBLEMS MUST BE overcome to reach a solution to the puzzle of UFOs and ETs. First, even when many people share the same experience, investigators often have only circumstantial evidence. People may see what *is* real, what they *think* is real, or what they wish to *believe* is real. This makes the reports difficult to evaluate. Next, if extraterrestrials are visiting the earth, their technology is far more advanced than ours. Earth science must play catch-up. Finally, people fear the unknown. Government and military agencies often believe it is safer to declare information secret or to explain UFOs as something else. This policy has also included what is called disinformation. This is information released to the public that is only partly true or completely misleading.

The most helpful change is open sharing of information. A step in this direction is the Freedom of Information Act, which became law in the United States in 1974. One group, Citizens Against UFO Secrecy (CAUS), has pressured government agencies to release many documents to the public. The released papers show that intelligence agencies, the FBI, and all U.S. military branches have considered the UFO question very important. Unfortunately, many documents have been so heavily censored that there is almost nothing left to read.

The UFO flap in Belgium is an example of open communication at work. Starting from the first reports in 1989, all branches of the Belgian government, the national police, civilian agencies, and scientists shared information. Nothing was marked *secret*, nothing was hidden, and there was no disinformation. Hopefully this can happen in other countries.

There are strong arguments against the validity of UFO experiences. One is that they are sometimes more like dreams than waking reality. For example, suppose you wake up to remember seeing a small gray being materialize through your bedroom wall, or you remember floating up into an extraterrestrial craft. The experience is so impossible it seems like a vivid dream.

Astrophysicist Carl Sagan believes that most such bizarre experiences can be classified as hallucinations. A hallucination is like a dream that has become as real as waking life. Just as people from the Middle Ages had visions of devils and flying witches, so people today have visions of strange creatures lifting them aboard

"There was some accident involving a UFO, and from there it varies greatly. There were occupants in each of the rumors that I have heard.... There are particular rumors [that] aren't necessarily from people who have been involved, but come from so many different sources it would lead you to believe it certainly is worth investigating a little further. My personal feeling all along...is...the government should be honest with the citizens of the United States, and they really underestimate the intelligence level of citizens of the country by continually hiding things from them."

Astronaut Gordon Cooper as quoted on "Factual Eyewitness Testimony of UFO Encounters," a 1978 record

flying saucers. Surely the many men and women who have come forward with tales of alien abduction are either remembering real events or have experienced an intense hallucination.

The solution may not be so simple. Some scientists suggest that what we call reality may be a projection—like the image on a television screen or the three-dimensional image produced by laser light shining through a hologram. Such projective realities could overlap like universes that intersect one another. A UFO might be from a reality that overlaps with ours. And the two realities could sometimes be out of sync, like a movie in which the words don't match people's lip movements. This theory might explain the time delay of the shadows cast on the disk by the group of people in Rendlesham Forest; the movements of the shadow could have appeared delayed by several seconds because two projective realities did not overlap perfectly. This might also explain Chuck Rak's perception that his alien examiners were "not the same frequency," as if he could not tune them in clearly.

The same theory might also account for the many reports that a UFO appeared instantly where there was nothing before, or that a UFO "winked out," only to reappear a few seconds later in another part of the sky. It is possible for intersections to move even faster than the speed of light, so if there are projective realities, there may also be "shortcuts" from one to another.

Scientists have searched deep space for extraterrestrial intelligence. Since we ourselves use electromagnetic waves to broadcast radio signals to and from our planetary probes, there might be radio signals reaching earth from distant civilizations. Astronomers have discovered planets circling other stars, as earth orbits our sun. Possibly a vast number of planetary systems in the universe include some planets rather like earth. For instance, a computer at the Harvard University observatory is linked to a radio telescope scanning the skies for such broadcasts. In 1994 astronomer Paul Horowitz reported that six signals from the middle of our Milky Way galaxy showed bursts typical of intelligent signals. However, some bursts would likely repeat their patterns, and thus far none has done so.

While this sky search is useful, it may be more important to understand the direct speechless communication mentioned in so many close encounter cases. The current situation is somewhat akin to a football quarterback looking for game signals from the overhead blimp rather than from the new player just sent in by the coach from the sidelines. Indeed, witness accounts to the Roswell incident and thousands of abduction cases suggest that an alien presence has already been here for some time.

Scientists also speculate on advanced propulsion. UFOs may fly by manipulating or neutralizing gravitational fields or by using antimatter as a power source. Earth technology has already made a start in this direction. And when more advances come, our own spacecraft may be able to duplicate maneuvers and speeds that are not possible today. Indeed, whether or not they are

real, UFO encounters stimulate earth science toward new achievements.

We are truly at the threshold of a new era. Remarkably, we are already preparing to accept, understand, and communicate with intelligent life from beyond our own small home in the universe.

(Opposite)
A radio telescope at the Harvard University observatory uses a computer to search for intelligent signals from outer space.

UFO ORGANIZATIONS

For more information, or to report a UFO sighting or an encounter experience, contact the following organizations:

The J. Allen Hynek Center for UFO Studies (CUFOS)
2457 Peterson Avenue
Chicago, IL 60659
312-271-3611

Mutual UFO Network (MUFON)
103 Oldtowne Road
Seguin, TX 78155-4099
210-379-9216

The UFO/ET World Traveling Museum and Library of
  Scientific Anomalies
Pat J. Marcattilio, Curator
138 Redfern Street
Trenton, NJ 08610
609-888-1358

BIBLIOGRAPHY

Berlitz, Charles, and William Moore. *The Roswell Incident.* New York: Grosset and Dunlap, 1980.

Fowler, Raymond E. *The Allagash Abductions.* Tigard, Oregon: Wild Flower, 1993.

———. *The Andreasson Affair.* Englewood Cliffs, New Jersey: Prentice-Hall, 1982.

Fuller, John G. *The Interrupted Journey.* New York: Dial, 1966.

Good, Timothy. *Alien Contact: Top-Secret UFO Files Revealed.* New York: Morrow, 1993.

Hoagland, Richard C. *The Monuments of Mars: A City on the Edge of Forever.* Berkley, California: North Atlantic, 1987.

Hopkins, Budd. *Intruders: The Incredible Visitations at Copley Woods.* New York: Random, 1987.

Hynek, J. Allen. *The Hynek UFO Report.* New York: Dell, 1977.

Jordan, Debbie, and Kathy Mitchell. *Abducted! The Story of Intruders Continues.* New York: Carrol & Graf, 1994.

Kettelkamp, Larry. *Investigating UFOs.* New York: Morrow, 1971.

Randle, Kevin D., and Donald R. Schmitt. *The Truth about the UFO Crash at Roswell.* New York: Avon, 1994.

Randles, Jenny. *From Out of the Blue.* New York: Berkley, 1993.

Webb, Walter N. *Encounter at Buff Ledge: A UFO Case History.* Chicago: J. Allen Hynek Center for UFO Studies, 1994.

INDEX

Illustrations in *italic*

INDEX